Praise for My Happy Place

'It's time to join our movement! Don't you want to design interior spaces consciously as well as beautifully too?! It is completely achievable. Let Rachel help you. Her book is an excellent support and reference material for anyone wishing to work with lower-impact materials – whether you are a designer or a design enthusiast. This book will save you hours of sourcing and you know that Rachel has quizzed the suppliers ready for you to start using.'

Chloe Bullock BIID RegID, BA (Hons), Materialise Interiors

my happy place

Healthy, sustainable and humane
interior design for life and work

RACHEL
FOWLER

First published in Great Britain by Practical Inspiration Publishing, 2021

ISBN   9781788602983 (print)
          9781788602976 (epub)
          9781788602969 (mobi)

Disclaimer
The product-related information included in this book has been kindly supplied by companies or is openly available and is correct at the time of writing. The author accepts no responsibility for the efficacy of referenced products with sustainability and animal-friendly tenets.

Author: Rachel Fowler
Website: www.rachelfowlerinteriors.com
Email: info@rachelfowlerinteriors.com
LinkedIn: www.linkedin.com/in/rachel-fowler-2aa620184
Instagram: www.instagram.com/rachelfowlerinteriors/

Contents

Preface

Sustainable living is more accessible than it has ever been before. A few years ago, ordering a vegan or vegetarian meal in a restaurant seemed like such a challenge. I remember that generally, when the food arrived, it didn't have much flavour and didn't look very appetizing. Times have changed though, and now there is a wide range of mouth-watering options that are as good for the planet as they are good for our bodies, making the choice to eat less meat much more accessible and appealing. I had this in mind when I was thinking about writing this book. I didn't want to write a book that feels like it is pointing a finger, or that makes non-vegans feel guilty and feel like they don't want to continue reading. Who likes being preached at?! No one.

There would be absolutely no point in me writing a book that alienates everybody apart from those who already think and act like me, especially if you believe, as I do, that caring for our planet, our bodies, and our health and happiness is a universal responsibility. Instead, I wanted to write a book that is easy to read and use; a book that could connect with anyone and everyone. This book is designed to be used by whoever picks it up, wherever they want to create a healthy, happy space – at home, at work, with a big or small budget, young or old, vegan or not.

In the following pages, I hope to show you that animal-friendly and sustainable interior designs can achieve the same stylish effects as designs which include non-sustainable materials. This book was made to be your go-to guide for achieving your design aspirations… which just happen to be eco-friendly, healthy and humane.

I know that searching for materials for a design project can sometimes feel like a nightmare, never-ending school project: just when you think you have cracked it, it uncovers additional questions. It can be even more of a challenge when you are trying to create sustainable and animal-friendly spaces. But that's what this book is for – think of it like a cheat-sheet to get you that A-grade home or workplace. I hope that you and your family will have lots of fun using it to create positive spaces, full of warmth, beauty and peace, which promote your health and wellbeing.

Before doing what I do now, I worked as a children's intensive care nurse. I loved nursing; it taught me a lot about myself and about how precious life is, and it took me all over the world. After 15 years, I decided that I wanted to fulfil my lifelong aspiration of working within the art and design world. So, I swapped scrubs for a sketch-pad, committed myself to full-time studying, and in June 2019 graduated with Honours from my Bachelor of Arts degree in Interior Design.

Introduction:
Sustainable and animal-friendly design

This book is not just another self-help guide on how to design and create amazing interiors. Its purpose is to act as a go-to guide in creating spaces – whether at home or in the office, inside or outside – which are both sustainable and animal friendly. This is particularly important in today's society due to effects that traditional methods have had on the environment and our health. For instance, the current air quality of internal spaces is considered to be poorer than that of the outside environment: including internal spaces within cities, where you would think that the outside environment would be worse. When designing a space, it is important to understand the effects that the materials we select can have – not just on the environment, but on our mental and physical wellbeing too.

This book is broken down into seven parts: one for each of the main elements used within the interior design process. These include: wall and floor coverings, furniture, lighting, fabric, and accessories. The final part looks at a room with a specific set of needs: how to create a healthy and humane infant nursery, which is a key question asked by many expecting mums and dads to be. Each part of the book explores why it is so important to include sustainable and humane choices in comparison to more traditional methods, and includes a resource guide for sourcing products as well as top tips on creating sustainable and humane designs.

Whether you're an amateur in this for the love, or a professional seeking to improve your practice, there will be something for you in here: it's been written with everyone in mind, from interior designers, architects and builders to DIY enthusiasts and students.

Sustainable design

So, what is sustainable design and why is it so important? Sustainable design involves designing your space in a manner which is not detrimental to the environment, both socially and economically. This means considering the full lifecycle of all products involved with the design and build process of a building, including:

- extraction of all raw materials out of the ground;
- manufacturing methods;
- transportation; and
- the end life (i.e. can it be re-used or recycled or is it biodegradable?).

The mindset for achieving sustainable design also involves a process called the circular economy. According to the Ellen MacArthur Foundation, the circular economy involves implementing into the design processes measures to eliminate waste; designing products whose components can be re-used time and time again; and changing the way we work and design so as to revitalize the earth's organic processes.

Animal-friendly design

I like to refer to vegan design as animal-friendly design. It's just about the word that works for you; personally, I know many people have negative associations with the word *vegan*. Or maybe it feels like too high a bar to set – you're not seeking to live a fully vegan lifestyle, perhaps, but that doesn't mean you're not interested in a humane interior.

Animal-friendly design, then, can be defined as designing in a way that is not to the detriment of any other living species. This means using materials which have not been tested on animals, and which contain no animal products or by-products. The good news is that availability of animal-friendly materials for the interior design industry is growing: for instance, leather alternatives are now being made from plant-based sources such as pineapple, mushroom and cork. Paints are being produced which aren't being tested on animals.

With this increased awareness and the need for animal-friendly and sustainable design, this is changing how designers and manufacturers think, design and produce products. However, do not just presume that all animal-friendly products are sustainable. Just because it is animal-friendly doesn't always make it a sustainable and a healthier option – keep an eye out for more specific guidance in the following pages.

I hope you find this book a useful reference guide in achieving healthy and humane designs.

Part One
Wall coverings

With lots of stylish choices, from wallpaper to ornate wood panelling, there is an abundance of wall coverings available when designing our homes or places of work. Wall coverings can add an injection of colour: from bright and bold hues to softer, neutral and earthy tones. However, it is important to remember that too many colours can overstimulate the senses, having a negative effect on our stress levels and wellbeing. Don't forget, too, that not everyone views a colour the same. For instance, interiors with white walls may be viewed by some people positively, as a Scandi design style. However, those same white walls may be viewed by others as too clinical, resembling something like the interior of a doctor's surgery.

Apart from colour, wall coverings can add texture and form to a design, taking away the plainness of bare walls and adding character and style. Think: does the wall covering you are choosing work with the design style and other materials selected to create it? Don't forget to take into consideration the positioning of the space: is it north or south facing? Does it have windows? The amount and type of light entering a space can affect how the colour of the wall coverings may look. Importantly, when selecting wall coverings for a design project, are the choices you are making sustainable and promoting the health and wellbeing of all those who will use the space?

When starting a design project, consider what the spaces you are designing are going to be used for. This is important so that you can create the correct ambience for each space: be creative and have some fun when selecting your wall coverings, but make sure it flows with all the other spaces. Are you a person who likes to read? One option could be to make use of these spare books by sticking them onto a wall with a plant-based wall adhesive, creating a feature wall. This looks great in places such as the toilet (gives your guests something to look at when they are in there), lounge, restaurants, hotels and libraries. Have a look at what's in your cupboards – you may find something which could look great as a wall covering.

Part One includes specific chapters on different types of wall coverings: paint, wallpaper, wood, natural stone, tiles, clay plaster, cork and Mogu Acoustic. Each short chapter will offer a brief description of what the product is, what makes it sustainable and animal friendly, and what it can add to your design scheme. There are also some top tips to consider when purchasing certain products and, wherever possible, some names of relevant suppliers.

Paint

Eco- and animal-friendly paints are important to help protect the environment and promote a healthy internal air quality, which ultimately promotes the health and wellbeing of both you and your family, work colleagues or clients. Conventional paints contain substances such as formaldehyde and volatile organic compounds (VOCs). VOCs are chemicals which, over time, release toxins into the environment; their use in paints is regulated but the regulations vary depending on where you live in the world. As well as containing VOCs, most traditional-style paints leave a thin membrane of plastic, which can trap damp, resulting in mould.

So, what makes a paint humane and eco-friendly? Supplier Edward Bulmer Paints suggests that a sustainable and humane paint is one 'which has no detrimental effect on the environment or society' (Edward Bulmer Paints, 2020). With that definition in mind, here are some top tips to consider when choosing your sustainable and animal-friendly paint.

> **Top tips: Paint**
>
> ➤ *Does the paint contain a low level of VOCs? Low VOC levels will help to promote a healthy internal air environment. All ingredients should be listed on the side of the tin, but if they're not, this information will be available from the manufacturer. Be aware of companies advertising their paint as VOC free; as the Earthborn Paints (2020) website advises, no paint is completely VOC free. However, paints can be low VOC, and this is generally preferable.*
>
> ➤ *Does it contain any animal products? Some paints contain casein (a milk protein), shellac (a resin from the female lac bug), or beeswax to act as a binder.*
>
> ➤ *Is the paint tested on animals? This information is available from the manufacturer.*
>
> ➤ *Think about the paint's carbon footprint. Consider the lifecycle of the paint, from creation to disposal. What has been the impact of the extraction and transportation of the raw materials that made the paint and container? What about the manufacturing and transportation of the item, and how the product can be disposed of?*

Painted walls, including ceilings, can add contrast, colour and texture to a space. For instance, a small room painted in lighter colours can make the space seem larger. Darker colours can radiate warmth and make a space seem smaller and cosier. Bright colours add a funky and upbeat vibe, whilst pastel tones can create a calming vibe. When choosing a colour scheme, ask yourself: will this flow throughout all of the spaces? Is it creating the design style you want? Also consider the location and positioning of the property. Natural light entering a space changes throughout the day and time of the year, which affects the ambience of a space. A north-facing room may get little or no direct sunlight, making it feel cooler, whereas south-facing rooms tend to be lighter and radiate a warmer feeling.

Suppliers

The companies listed here are considered to be animal-friendly and sustainable paint suppliers. This list is accurate as of the time of writing this book.

Auro Natural Clay Paint

Available in the United Kingdom, Europe, Middle East, United States, Canada and Asia.

Earthborn Paints

Located in the United Kingdom.

Currently available in the United Kingdom, Europe and the United States.

Please note: Earthborn Casein Paint is, at the time of writing this book, not animal friendly.

Figure 1.0
Image provided by Earthborn Paints

Figure 1.1
Image provided by Earthborn Paints

Figure 1.2
Image provided by Earthborn Paints

Edward Bulmer Paints

Located in the United Kingdom.

Available in the United Kingdom and Europe.

Figure 1.3
Image provided by Edward Bulmer Paints

Figure 1.4
Image provided by Edward Bulmer Paints

Eico

Available in the United Kingdom.

Paint manufactured by using 100% geothermal and hydro-power energy.

Francesca's Paints Ltd

Located in the United Kingdom.

Available in the United Kingdom.

> 'I am the #theColourwoman'. Creating colours using natural paints and colour matching gives me joy. I discovered the world of traditional paints when I was living in Australia in the 90s, by pure chance, I didn't know anything about it. I worked with a fantastic paint manufacturer and I immediately fell in love with the world of colour mixing and making paint. After 7 years with them, I came back to London in 1996 and opened Francesca's Paints. Each colour that I make has a story. We hand mix every tin of paint. Our colour charts are hand painted. It is a work of love. I am #theColourwoman.

Francesca Wezel

Figure 1.5
Image provided by Francesca's Paints Ltd

Graphenstone

Headquarters located in Spain.

Available in the United Kingdom, Europe, Australia, China, South Korea, Japan, India, New Zealand, Singapore, Vietnam, Canada, the United States, Costa Rica, Panama, Mexico, Bolivia, Colombia, Chile, Ecuador and Peru.

Pure & Original

Headquarters located in the Netherlands.

Available globally from Europe to the United States and China.

Figure 1.6
Image provided by Pure & Original

Kids room with blue bench:
Photographer and stylist: Iris Floor
Wall: Paint quality: Fresco
Colour: Bohemian Vintage

Wooden basket:
Paint quality: Fresco
Colour: Dry Terra

Bench:
Paint quality: Traditional Paint
Colour: Blue (applied with an old look)

Figure 1.7
Image provided by Pure & Original

Flatlay:
Colour: Chalky Coral
Paint quality: Licetto washable paint
Photographer: Margaret de Lange
Stylist: Kirsten Visdal
Design: KOI Colour Studio

Wallpaper

Like paints, there is an array of wallpaper companies offering many different types and styles. The same principles for choosing a humane and healthy paint apply to wallpaper too: selecting a product that promotes health and wellbeing, creates a healthy internal air environment, and has a positive lifecycle (biodegradable).

Sustainable and animal-friendly wallpaper can be made from a huge variety of sources and materials: paper sourced from sustainable forests, linen, seagrass, mica, cork, water-based paints, grass-cloth, organic fibres such as coconut bark, Japanese paper and sequoia bark. I have just developed my own range of sustainable wallpaper. I have specially selected a manufacturer whose processes include using electricity from renewable sources. My designs are printed on paper that is harvested from Forest Stewardship Council (FSC) certified forests, with no hidden extras. My wallpaper uses non-toxic (confirmed by the manufacturer), water-based ink and is not coated in any harmful finishes. Non-woven wallpaper, even though it can be FSC certified, may contain plastic, increasing its negative impact on sustainability. In June 2020, an Italian company called Glamora launched a new type of sustainable wallpaper made from a mix of new and recycled linen and cellulose fibres.

Figure 1.8
An example of paperweave wallpaper by Mark Alexander
Image provided by Mark Alexander

Figure 1.9
An example of grass-cloth wallpaper by Mark Alexander
Image provided by Mark Alexander

Figure 2.0
An example of Japanese paper wallpaper by Mark Alexander
Image provided by Mark Alexander

Top tips: Choosing a sustainable and animal-friendly wallpaper

➢ *Is the paper sourced from sustainable forests or recycled paper?*

➢ *What paints are used in creating patterns? These should be water-based paints if at all possible.*

➢ *Does it contain vinyl? Sustainable wallpaper should not contain any vinyl as this is a non-biodegradable material.*

➢ *Consider the wallpaper's carbon footprint – how have the materials and the product travelled, been sourced or impacted the environment in the manufacture, supply, use or disposal?*

➢ *Look for a wallpaper that does not contain polyvinyl chloride (PVC). PVC can produce VOCs, creating a negative effect on your internal air quality and your health.*

➢ *What is it packaged in?*

➢ *Ensure VOC-free and animal-friendly adhesives are used for hanging the wallpaper.*

➢ *If in doubt, double check with the supplier that it is animal friendly.*

➢ *Non-woven wallpaper can contain plastic.*

Wallpaper can be used not just on walls but on several surfaces: for instance, ceilings, wardrobe doors and ornate wooden panelling. It can add contrast, colour and texture, whilst reflecting light around the space. In addition, wallpaper can add character and glamour, and create vibrant spaces. Wallpaper comprising vertical stripes can make a space with low ceilings look higher – remember to get extra paper for pattern-matching if necessary!

Suppliers

Glamora – GlamPure range

Located in Italy.

Available globally.

The wallpaper is made from a mix of new and recycled linen and cellulose fibres. A special paste is needed, provided by Glamora, which is also sustainable and animal friendly.

Figure 2.1
Kokoro wallpaper
Image provided by Glamora

Figure 2.2
Temps Perdu wallpaper
Image provided by Glamora

Figure 2.3
Interplay wallpaper
Image provided by Glamora

Rachel Fowler Interiors

Located in the United Kingdom.

Available globally.

Figure 2.4
Leopards wallpaper
Rachel Fowler Interiors

Figure 2.5
Japanese Cranes – Boogie Nights wallpaper
Rachel Fowler Interiors

Wood

Wooden wall coverings come in an array of styles. You've got everything from traditional – for example, Georgian or Regency panelling – to more modern, decorative and exuberant designs. Back in the 1800s, wooden wall coverings were used to protect the walls. Nowadays, within interior design, it is considered to be more of a decorative feature.

There are two types of wood available for wall covering: softwood and hardwood. Softwood, such as pine, is less durable than a hardwood like oak. According to Urbanline Architectural (2018), though, softwood is easier to work with than a hardwood, and tends to be cheaper. There is also the option of using recycled wood, available from most salvage yards. Most woods are available globally, but availability may vary depending upon your location. Another great feature of including wooden wall coverings is that it can help insulate a space, decreasing the amount of heat lost, acting as a form of insulation. Therefore, this can help reduce a property's energy consumption.

Wood is recognized as a sustainable product in almost all forms, due to its lifecycle. Trees are a natural and renewable product, which can last for long periods of time. At its end of life, wood can be recycled or it can be broken down and put back into the soil. Some virgin wood sources are more sustainable than others; for example, some companies are now using mango wood due to its sustainable regrowth properties. However, it must be noted that not all wood sold is classed as sustainable. Wood which is sourced from sustainable forests is marked with the letters FSC (Forest Stewardship Council). If this mark is not present, it must be presumed that the wood is not from a sustainable source.

> **Top tips: Wooden wall coverings**
>
> ➤ *Look for the FSC logo.*
>
> ➤ *Check out reclamation yards.*
>
> ➤ *Ensure all adhesives used in fitting the wooden wall covering are VOC free.*
>
> ➤ *Ensure that all paints or lacquers used to finish off the wooden wall coverings are animal friendly and low VOC.*

Wooden wall coverings add character, warmth, texture and form. They break up the plainness of bare walls whilst adding depth to your design. In addition, wood can be used as a decorative covering for ceilings, such as those used originally in Chinese interior design. In particular, wooden ceilings are a great concept and feature to consider when designing restaurants. It can help you achieve a traditional-style design or a more upbeat modern/contemporary look.

Suppliers

Encore Reclamation

Located in the United Kingdom.

Contact supplier for availability.

Scumble Goosie

Located in the United Kingdom.

Available in the United Kingdom.

Figure 2.6
Image provided by Scumble Goosie (manufacturer of wooden furniture)
English Panelling Company
https://scumblegoosie.co.uk
www.englishpanelling.com

Figure 2.7
Image provided by Scumble Goosie (manufacturer of wooden furniture)
English Panelling Company
https://scumblegoosie.co.uk
www.englishpanelling.com

Natural stone

Natural stone creates unique, opulent and exuberant spaces. Marble, a natural stone, has been used in interiors since Roman times. Natural stone is an organic and sustainable material. Found in various locations around the world, it is excavated from the earth and requires no additional by-products in its manufacturing process – although you should ensure that VOC-free products are used in the installation. Natural stone is long-lasting, which means it does not need replacing often, and even considering the cost of marble and transportation of the material, the long-term benefits will outweigh the costs. Natural stone can be recycled or put back into the ground at its end of life. Some natural stones require sealing with a sealant due to being highly porous. This can affect the sustainability of the natural stone, if the sealant used contains chemicals. Look for an alternative, or make sure that whoever is laying the floor uses an eco-friendly product, containing no chemicals.

Natural stone comes in an array of different textures, colours and detailing, making it a very versatile product. It is recognized that the materials used to create a space can affect us emotionally, especially a person's level of anxiety, and natural stone can add calmness and a positive energy to a design. Natural stone can be sourced from any reputable supplier globally.

Marble

Marble complements most spaces in your home or places of work, including bathrooms, kitchens, hallways, stairs and dining rooms.

Slate

Slate comes in a variety of different hues from pale grey to black. Its variations in colour can add texture and contrast to a design. Its surface can be uneven, but it is a great option in areas which have heavy traffic flow. Slate wall coverings work especially well in the design of residential properties: for instance, in bathrooms and kitchens.

Limestone/travertine

Travertine is formed by minerals from springs. It is great in areas such as hallways, kitchens and bathrooms.

Top tips: Natural stone

➤ *Think about the product's lifecycle; buy from a reputable local stockist where possible. Could you source the natural stone from a reclamation yard?*

➤ *Check to see if it has been sealed in any finishes which may contain chemicals.*

➤ *What space are you using it in? Will the natural stone you are selecting be suitable for that space?*

➤ *Cost: check this out before you finalize your design. Though marble may be expensive, think about the product's longevity.*

➤ *Will it complement your design?*

➤ *Buy enough natural stone to account for any breakages when laying the flooring.*

➤ *Use a healthy, humane and eco-friendly certified sealant, tile adhesive and grout.*

Suppliers

Corradini Group

Located in Italy.

Contact supplier for availability.

Salvatori

Located in Italy.

Contact supplier for availability.

Mandarin Stone

Located in the United Kingdom.

Available in the United Kingdom.

Figure 2.8
Calacatta Amber Honed Marble
Image provided by Mandarin Stone

Tiles

When searching for the correct style, colour and size of a tile for your design project, it won't be long before you realize that there is an abundance of manufacturers and suppliers. Most people select tiles for their kitchens, bathrooms and outside dining areas – although you are by no means limited to these spaces. When choosing your wall tiles, as with other wall coverings, the important thing is to think about what style and ambience you are trying to create. What colour tile would complement the other materials chosen for your design project? Dark colours can make a space look small and cold, whilst too much white can make a space look too clinical. How will the space be lit? For bathrooms, do the tiles help create that serene and meditative space which will help you to unwind at the end of each day?

Tiles can add an injection of colour and break up the bareness of walls, whilst adding form and texture to a design. In addition, you can create eye-catching designs using the same or different shaped and coloured tiles. Tiles are a great option when designing both commercial and residential properties.

Ceramic tiles

Ceramic tiles are sustainable because they're made of sand clay and other natural substances. In addition, Conestoga Tile (2015) writes that it is not a difficult job to extract the materials used to create the tiles – meaning it is less impactful to the planet in production. Ceramic tiles are made from a much coarser clay than porcelain tiles, and contain only a small amount of kaolin clay. They have strong heat-resistance properties, making them a good option for countertops. Ceramic tiles are also a good option for wall coverings in areas less exposed to water. They come in an array of styles and colours to complement your chosen design and at the end of life, they can be smashed up and recycled.

Porcelain tiles

Porcelain tiles contain a special type of clay: kaolin. The tiles are considered to be much denser in comparison to ceramic tiles, making them more hardwearing. Additionally, porcelain tiles are more water resistant than ceramic tiles, making them a better option for walls in areas such as bathrooms and wet-rooms. They come in an array of different styles ranging from contemporary through to wood effect. Porcelain tiles have a positive lifecycle from extraction to end of life (tiles can be smashed up and recycled).

Recycled glass mosaic tiles

Recycled glass mosaic tiles are made from discarded glass, such as used bottles. The glass is sorted out into various colours and then melted down to form tiles. The advantages of selecting this kind of tile include: they are easy to clean and do not stain; there is an array of coloured tiles to choose from; and they can throw back light around the space. Check online for your nearest local supplier.

Cotto tiles

Cristina Celestino, Creative Director at Fornace Brioni, notes, 'Cotto is made exclusively from clay and rainwater' – this makes Cotto tiles eco-friendly in both production and use. They can be recycled, and at Fornace Brioni they are made by hand, meaning that the lifecycle is very low impact and positive from beginning to end.

Recycled tiles

Just like the majority of things these days, you can buy recycled or reclaimed tiles. These can come from anywhere in the world: Mediterranean countries, for example, are a rich source of recycled tiles. Maitland and Poate, a company based in London who sell recycled tiles, state that 'our tiles are old and made from cement, sand and marble dust as well as natural pigments'.

Tiles made from recycled raw materials

Fireclay (based in the United States) produce tiles made from recycled clay and covered in a lead-free glaze. The company offers a range of tiles made from recycled materials. The tiles can add charm, inject colour and come in a variety of shapes and sizes. The company delivers globally.

Top tips: Tiles

> ➤ *Ensure your choice of tile is suitable for that type of space.*
>
> ➤ *Check that the finish of the tile (glaze) does not contain any harmful chemicals.*
>
> ➤ *Check what type of pigments have been used to colour the tiles. Do these comprise natural materials?*
>
> ➤ *Think about the lifecycle: can you buy it from a local supplier?*
>
> ➤ *Buy enough tiles to account for any breakages when laying the floor.*
>
> ➤ *Use a healthy, humane and eco-friendly certified tile adhesive and grout.*

As with natural stone, ceramic, recycled glass mosaic and Cotto tiles have a positive effect on both internal and external air quality, creating a healthy and humane environment. However, if the adhesives and grout used to fix the tiles onto the wall are not VOC free, this can have a negative effect on the internal or external air quality.

Suppliers

Fireclay

Located in the United States.

Available worldwide.

Fornace Brioni Cotto (Cotto tiles)

Located in Italy.

Available worldwide.

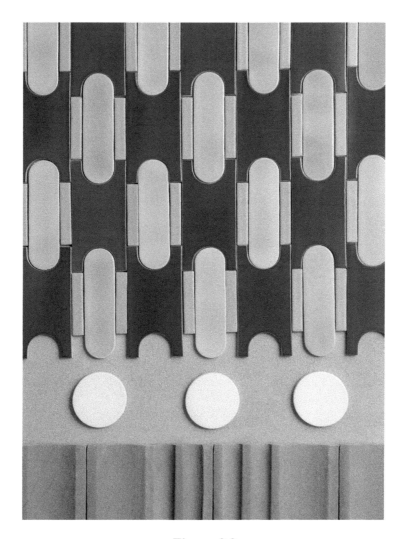

Figure 2.9
Image provided by Fornace Brioni
Photo credits: Mattia Balsamini
Design and creative direction by Cristina Celestino

In the picture above:
Giardino all'Italiana – Tivoli – Wall covering
Giardino delle delizie – Delizie – Wall covering
Gonzaga – Alberti – Wall covering

Figure 3.0
Image provided by Fornace Brioni
Photo credits: Mattia Balsamini
Design and creative direction by Cristina Celestino

In the picture above:
Gonzaga – Alberti – Wall covering
Gonzaga – Te – Flooring

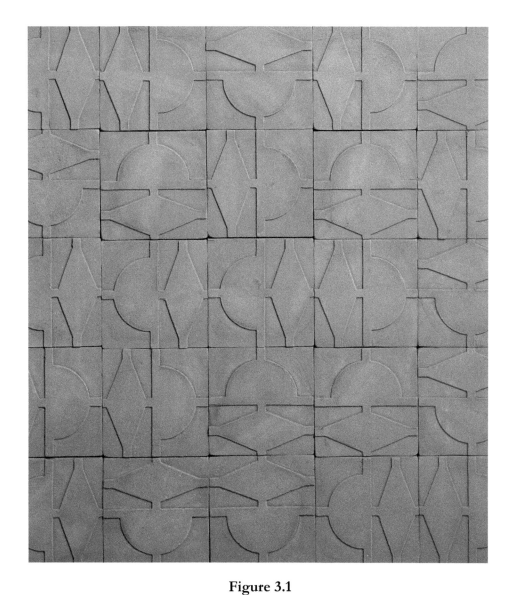

Figure 3.1
Image provided by Fornace Brioni
Photo credits: Mattia Balsamini
Design and creative direction by Cristina Celestino

In the picture above:
Giardino all'Italiana – Acanti V00 – Wall covering

Figure 3.2
Image provided by Fornace Brioni
Photo credits: Mattia Balsamini
Design and creative direction by Cristina Celestino

In the picture above:
A selection of variegated Cotto material samples

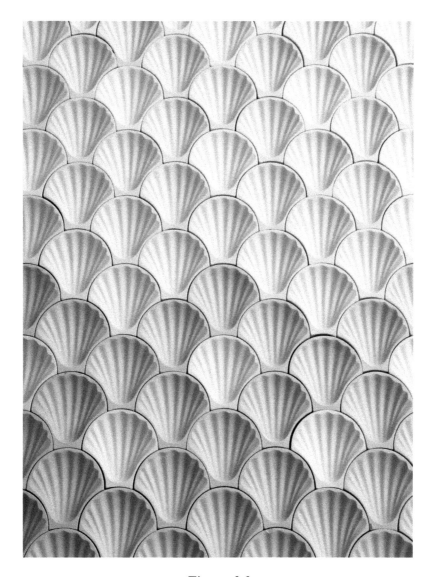

Figure 3.3
Image provided by Fornace Brioni
Photo credits: Mattia Balsamini
Design and creative direction by Cristina Celestino

In the picture above:
Giardino delle delizie – Rocaille – Wall covering

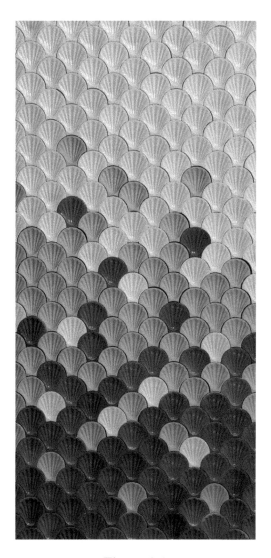

Figure 3.4
Image provided by Fornace Brioni
Photo credits: Mattia Balsamini
Design and creative direction by Cristina Celestino

In the picture above:
Giardino delle delizie – Rocaille – Wall covering
A mix of glossy and Cotto tiles

Iris Ceramica (porcelain and ceramic)

Located in Italy.

Available worldwide.

Figure 3.5
Blocks Collection
Image provided by Iris Ceramica

Figure 3.6
Marmi Collection
Image provided by Iris Ceramica

Figure 3.7
LOL Collection
Image provided by Iris Ceramica

Figure 3.8
LOL Collection
Image provided by Iris Ceramica

Maitland and Poate Recycled Tiles

Located in the United Kingdom.

Available worldwide.

Figure 3.9
Image provided by Maitland and Poate
www.maitlandandpoate.com
Photographer: Jacqui Melville

Figure 4.0
Image provided by Maitland and Poate
www.maitlandandpoate.com
Photographer: Malcolm Menzies

Figure 4.1
Image provided by Maitland and Poate
www.maitlandandpoate.com
Photographer: Jacqui Melville

Clay plaster

A clean, minimalist and natural-looking wall covering, clay plaster is made from natural clay, minerals and pigments. It has a positive lifecycle from extraction to manufacturing, which produces no waste, to end of life, as it's recyclable and compostable. VOC and formaldehyde free, clay plaster wall coverings create healthy and breathable spaces for you and your family. In addition, clay plaster walls can absorb any unwanted noise, whilst helping to regulate heating within a space. It is available in an array of finishes, from smooth to textured.

Clay plaster can help create a calming, peaceful and tranquil ambience. It can be used in the design of shops, hospitality and residential properties. The earthy tones and composition emanate positive vibes, whilst promoting the health and wellbeing of all those who use the space.

Top tips: Clay plaster

➤ *Is it suitable for the space you are designing?*

➤ *Contact Clayworks directly for the wall covering.*

Supplier

Clayworks

Located in the United Kingdom.

Available worldwide.

Figure 4.2
Image by Taran Wilkhu, courtesy of Clayworks

Figure 4.3
Bamford Spa
Photographer: Edmund Sumner, courtesy of Clayworks

Cork

People generally think of cork as something that pops out of a good bottle of wine. However, cork has been used in interiors since at least 1904, and is well worth considering as a wall covering. Cork comes from the bark of a cork oak tree. The removal of the bark does not compromise the life or health of the trees as it is able to re-grow – this already makes cork a sustainable material, but even better, cork interior products are made from the leftovers of the wine cork industry, making it actually a re-purposed waste material. Cork's natural composition creates a toxin-free and eco-friendly space. It can last up to 50 years, is biodegradable and promotes a clean, healthy and humane environment.

Cork is aesthetically pleasing and can absorb unwanted noise – which is great if you have a busy household. In addition, cork can help insulate a space, making a room more energy efficient, and it is also waterproof. Cork wall covering is available in tiles, including geometric styles. It is also available in a number of colours – but do double check with the supplier that coloured cork tiles do not contain any toxins or added chemicals. Cork can create a warm and minimalist design. It will add texture, form and colour and is available globally. Remember, the products used for installing the cork tiles should be VOC free.

Top tips: Cork

➢ *Is cork suitable for the space?*

➢ *Think lifecycle: buy from a reputable local eco-friendly stockist where possible.*

➢ *Check what pigments have been used to colour the cork. Are these natural products, chemical free?*

➢ *Use a healthy, humane and eco-friendly certified adhesive for the installation of cork wall tiles/blocks.*

Supplier

Puretree Cork – Organic Blocks

Located in the United Kingdom.

Contact supplier for further information.

Mogu Acoustic – Mycelium-based acoustic/ sound-absorbing panels for walls and ceilings

Mogu, an Italian based, innovation-driven, design company, has created and commercialized a collection of acoustic panels for walls and ceiling application, having as main constituent selected fungal mycelium, the 'vegetative' stage of mushrooms. The related bio-fabrication process involves growing mycelium on 'pre-engineered, residual fibres, coming from other value chains, such as the agro-industry and the manufacturing/textile industry'. This may sound jargon, but to put it in simple words, the company grows its 'mushrooms' on low-value residues from other industrial processes, such as for instance discarded cotton fibres. The process implemented for producing Mogu Acoustic panels does not require any plastic or any of its derivatives. The acoustic tiles are completely biodegradable at the end of their life, and fully tested and certified by recognized third-party laboratories, as allergens-free and VOC-free (Volatile Organic Compounds' emissions close to none), among others. Furthermore, Mogu Acoustic tiles are durable and easy to install. They are naturally antistatic, meaning that they will not collect large amounts of dust. All in all, this is something of a super-product in terms of true sustainability and animal friendliness, making it a great option for designing interiors, such as for instance office spaces, through aesthetically unique and beautiful indoor panels, embedding advanced technical features that will help absorb unwanted sounds.

Top tips: Mushroom (mycelium-based) acoustic-absorbing panels for wall and ceiling applications

> ➢ *Contact Mogu directly for acoustic-absorbent panels for wall and ceiling applications.*

> ➢ *Will it work with the space you are designing?*

Supplier

Mogu

Located in Italy.

Available worldwide.

Figure 4.4
Image provided by Mogu

Figure 4.5
Image provided by Mogu

Figure 4.6
Image provided by Mogu

Part Two
Floor coverings

What do you like to feel under your feet? Are you a person who likes that soft feeling of carpet, or do you prefer the smooth coolness of a wooden floor? Of course, which room you are sourcing flooring for will influence the choices you make. For instance, a typical choice of flooring for a bathroom, which needs to be water resistant and easy to clean, might be tiles (porcelain) or a natural stone (marble).

As with wall coverings, you want to ask yourself whether the flooring complements the other materials you have selected, not just for this design but throughout all the spaces concerned. What is the volume of traffic passing through the space and do you have any pets? For spaces with a high volume of traffic or people who have pets, certain products may not be suitable due to their lack of durability. On the other hand, some flooring products can help with the absorption of unwanted noise and can further help insulate a space, which may be good for high-traffic or animal-populated areas. Flooring can add texture whilst softening an otherwise stark design. Be creative with the type of flooring you select. Add some colour, or levels.

The products included within this part of the book overlap with some of those featured in Part One, 'Wall coverings'. Part Two includes information on the following types of flooring: wood, bamboo, palm wood, natural stone, tiles, carpet and rugs, cork, natural linoleum, Mogu and Foresso.

Wood

As we know from looking at wood as a wall covering, there are two main categories of wood to consider for flooring – softwood, which is easier to work with, and hardwood, which is more durable. There are also wood-type materials, such as bamboo and palm wood, that don't fit neatly into these categories – we will come to these later.

Softwood trees are less dense than hardwood trees. They come from the conifer tree family: for instance, fir, pine, spruce and yew are all softwoods. Typically, pine is the choice of softwood for flooring. Softwood is cheaper than hardwood: it grows quicker, making it ostensibly more sustainable – but as we now know, it is not as durable, which may mean it would have to be replaced sooner and more often. This, of course, has an impact on the sustainability of a floor. Softwood availability will depend upon location within the world, but it can generally be sourced from a reputable timber merchant. It has a positive lifecycle from cradle to grave. Softwood flooring adds warmth and character to a design. This type of flooring is typically used in Scandinavian-style interiors.

A hardwood comes from the deciduous tree family, which is slow growing. This includes oak, maple, cherry, rosewood, walnut and ash. When it comes to hardwood flooring, oak is generally the preferred option. Hardwood flooring can add value to your property; it is seen as desirable, mostly because it is more durable than softwood flooring. It's a good option for areas within your home or work with increased levels of traffic. Hardwood is long-lasting, having a positive effect on the product's lifecycle. In addition, it can be re-used or put back into the ground at the end of its life. Hardwood flooring comes in a variety of styles from parquet, herringbone or just straight planks. It creates an upmarket design, complementing a variety of design styles, for instance modern to art-deco. Hardwood flooring's availability will depend upon location within the world, but it can usually be sourced from reputable flooring specialists or timber merchants.

When purchasing any wooden flooring, ensure it has the Forest Stewardship Council (FSC) logo on it. The FSC is a global organization which 'promotes responsible management of the world's forests'. This means the wood is sustainably sourced.

Of course, wood cannot be left raw, otherwise it would wear away too quickly – it needs a finish of some kind. So, when finishing the flooring, ensure you select a product which is healthy and humane. For instance, Auro Floor varnish (267). Auro states that their floor varnish is made from 'naturally occurring raw materials, plastic free, child and pet safe and comes in recyclable packaging'. Natural products are generally considered to have a lower level of VOCs, therefore promoting a healthier internal air quality.

Why not add a thin ornate wooden border or corner edging to the flooring? This will create a more unique and sophisticated-looking floor.

Reclaimed wood

Wood that has been removed from older properties, for instance residential or commercial properties, is known as reclaimed wood. Using reclaimed wood, especially if it is reclaimed hardwood, is not only a very eco-friendly option but can add value to your property. Though it may not be FSC-sourced wood – there's usually no way of telling, as the FSC mark may well have been removed or covered in the original use – it is still considered a sustainable option due to the wood being recycled. When buying reclaimed wood, look out for signs of any unwanted visitors such as wood-worm or termites. Free of these pests, reclaimed wood is usually a durable choice of flooring. However, it is not recommended for use within bathrooms because it is more susceptible to the constant steam and damp, which can cause the wood to crack and swell. Reclaimed hardwood can be more expensive than cheap, new softwood – but the long-term benefits will usually outweigh the cost. Reclaimed wooden floors can create a vintage style whilst adding character, warmth and a natural feeling to a design. Reclaimed wood can be sourced worldwide from restoration yards.

If you are going to include reclaimed wood, or even simply use existing floorboards within the property, be careful when restoring them. The varnishes, lacquers or paints that you remove can, when sanding the boards, emit gases and dust which can be harmful if inhaled. Ensure you are working in a space with adequate ventilation, take frequent breaks, wear personal protective equipment (PPE) such as a mask and goggles, and keep the room well ventilated after finishing work for several days.

Bamboo flooring

Bamboo flooring is not actually wood but is made from the woody grass of the bamboo plant. It has its own unique and distinctive grain pattern. The bamboo is generally grown in Asia, and is considered to be harder wearing than oak flooring, making it suitable for areas of mid to high levels of traffic. It is water resistant, therefore decreasing the possibility of mould or mildew. It is considered to be a good flooring to install for those with allergies due to it being inhospitable to dust mites. Bamboo is a sustainable plant which has the ability to grow back within three to five years. Harvesting involves the stalk being cut whilst the plant's roots remain in the ground, enabling it to re-grow without having to re-plant any seeds. Lewis Bamboo (2020) writes: 'A grove of bamboo release 35 percent more oxygen than an equivalent stand of trees.'

There are companies around the world who sell bamboo flooring; however, not all of the bamboo flooring sold comes from sustainably sourced forests. In addition, some manufacturing processes may include the use of chemicals. I recommend when purchasing this product to opt for the high-end bamboo flooring because it is generally understood that the high-end manufacturers of bamboo flooring implement better practices for sustainability. Bamboo flooring looks great in the design of hotels and is a great alternative to traditional wooden flooring in the home and office.

Bamboo flooring can come in a number of different colours and finishes. It can be used in the majority of spaces within your home, from kitchen to bathroom. An advantage of bamboo flooring is it can be used for the flooring within a shower. However, the flooring must be treated with the correct finish. Bamboo flooring is very versatile, complementing an array of different design styles: for instance, contemporary, rustic or modern. It can add warmth, depth and style to your design. As with wooden flooring, it can be fitted as plain planks or you can create a design such as chevrons.

Palm wood

Palm wood flooring is made from palm trees which cannot bear coconuts anymore. Traditionally, once a coconut tree had stopped bearing fruit, it was felled and the trunks were just discarded. It's not regulated by the FSC because coconut is considered an agricultural product rather than a forestry product, but it is nonetheless considered to be an eco-friendly material. It is durable and hardwearing – so a good alternative to hardwood – but it is quicker to grow than deciduous trees, making it slightly more sustainable. Just like all the other types of wood featured in Part Two, as long as no chemicals have been used in the manufacturing process, palm wood can either be re-used or put back into the soil as biodegradable waste.

Palmwood is available in a number of different finishes, for instance flat grain, edge grain, sugar deco and red palm. Furthermore, it can be finished in several different-coloured lacquers. Palm wood flooring adds contrast, creating elegant spaces within your home. It complements different design styles, such as contemporary or rustic. To soften up the design, add some ornate rugs. Palm wood is available from select global suppliers.

Top tips: Wood, bamboo or palm wood flooring

➤ *Is the wood sustainably sourced? Has it got the FSC logo?*

➤ *Can you source it locally?*

➤ *Identify what has been used to finish the wood (lacquer, stain etc.).*

➤ *Can you salvage any of the existing floorboards within the space(s)?*

➤ *Could you use wood from a reclamation yard instead of buying new?*

➤ *Select animal-friendly and sustainable products for finishing the flooring.*

➤ *Great product to use in the design of residential or commercial properties.*

➤ *Make sure any gaps within your wooden floors are filled to prevent any loss of heat in the cooler months.*

➤ *You can use rugs to soften a design which includes wooden flooring.*

➤ *Identify all the ingredients used in manufacturing, such as the glues and finishes, especially in bamboo flooring. Some products used in the manufacturing of bamboo flooring use urea formaldehyde, which is a toxic chemical.*

Suppliers

Hargreaves Reclaimed Wood Flooring

Located in Scotland.

Contact supplier for availability.

Lassco Wooden Flooring

Located in the United Kingdom.

Contact supplier for availability.

Reclaimed Flooring Company

Located in the United Kingdom and New York.

Contact supplier for availability.

For bamboo and palm wood, check for a locally sustainable and eco-friendly certified company.

Natural stone

Natural stone can create healthy and humane spaces at home or at work. Its extraction from the ground is simpler than a complex or harmful sourcing process; it does not require any additional products in its manufacturing process; and at the end of its life, it can be recycled or put back into the ground. As identified in Part One, some natural stone will require being sealed with a sealant. Ensure that the sealant selected is eco-friendly: you may need to contact the company directly for this information.

Slate

Mined from different locations around the world, slate is available internationally. Its variations in colour can add texture and contrast to a design. Its surface can be uneven but is a great option in areas which have heavy flows of traffic as it is very hardwearing – making it also a great choice of flooring if you have pets. Slate flooring works especially well in bathrooms, hallways and kitchens as it's water resistant and easy to clean. When laying a slate floor, consider using a sustainable grey grout. Slate flooring complements an array of designs, including modern to traditional. It creates elegant and harmonious designs.

Marble

Probably one of the most expensive types of natural stone flooring, marble is extracted from a number of mines located around the globe. If you can afford to use marble then its durability and sustainable properties far outweigh its cost. Marble flooring can be used in areas of high volumes of traffic and is pet friendly. Be careful though – it provides a smooth surface, which can become slippery when wet. Marble flooring comes in several different colours and detailing. Marble complements most areas within residential and commercial properties, including bathrooms, kitchens, hallways, stairs and dining rooms. It creates luxurious and timeless designs.

Limestone

A natural product, which is mined worldwide. Limestone does not require any additional products in its manufacturing and is easily extracted out of the ground. Limestone comes in slabs, which can vary in colour and evenness of surface from one piece to another. However, this will add texture and intrigue to your floors. One such type of limestone is travertine, formed by minerals from springs. Limestone can complement both modern and traditional design styles. It is a great flooring option for the home; for instance, it works very well in hallways, kitchens and bathrooms.

Top tips: Stone flooring

➢ *Ensure all tile sealant, adhesive and grout is eco-friendly and humane, promoting the health and wellbeing of you and your family.*

➢ *Buy enough natural stone to account for any breakages when laying the flooring.*

➢ *Think about the lifecycle of the natural stone. Can you source it locally?*

Suppliers

Mandarin Stone

Located in the United Kingdom.

Available in the United Kingdom.

Salvatori

Located in Italy.

Contact supplier for availability.

Figure 4.7
Nero Riven Slate
Image provided by Mandarin Stone

Figure 4.8
Porcini Emperador Honed Marble
Image provided by Mandarin Stone

Tiles

As we saw in Part One, tiles are great for injecting colour and creating grand designs. They're available in a variety of sizes and shapes, making them adaptable for both small and large areas. They are great for areas of high volumes of traffic and pets as they're hardwearing and easy to keep clean. Tiles can add elegance and beauty to a design. The majority of tiles are made from natural clay, therefore protecting other resources from issues such as deforestation. A tile's finish, however, is generally made from glaze. Traditionally, the glaze used for finishing tiles consisted of noxious substances. However, Tile Devil (2018) writes, 'a wide range of non-hazardous glazes are now readily available'. This information should be available from the supplier if not included on a box of tiles. The materials used in creating tiles are available from numerous locations around the world. Therefore, tiles are considered to have a low carbon footprint.

Porcelain

Porcelain tiles are made from a special mixture of clay, which is different to the mix used in ceramic tiles. Porcelain tiles are considered to be much denser in comparison to ceramic tiles, making them more hardwearing. Porcelain tiles come in an array of different styles and designs. For instance, their design can imitate natural products such as wood or marble. Porcelain tiles can create clean lines within a design, complementing both modern and contemporary interiors, and helping you to add some elegance to your hotel, restaurant or home design.

Ceramic

Ceramic tiles are made from a much coarser clay. The tiles are fired in a kiln at a lower temperature than porcelain, making them more sustainable in terms of production impact. However, they can be more prone to water penetration and are less hardwearing than porcelain, so they may not last as long or be suitable for all areas.

Terracotta

Terracotta means 'bakes earth' in Italian. It can be considered a sustainable tile due to being made from clay, a natural product, which has a high iron content. Terracotta tiles are known for being permeable (absorbent). If considered, it's recommended that some kind of glaze or finish is applied to help decrease the absorption of water or other liquids. It can be used both internally and externally. Its reddish-orange tone adds warmth to a design, making it ideal for rustic or Mediterranean design styles in both residential and commercial properties. Available from global tile stockists.

Reclaimed/recycled

Nowadays, there is the option of reclaimed/recycled tiles. Bert & May's (based in the United Kingdom) recycled tile range includes everything from patterned to plain terracotta tiles. Fireclay (based in the United States, available globally) recycled tiles consist of recycled granite fines and are covered in a lead-free glaze. All tiles made by Fireclay are hand-made and made to order. Recycled tiles can be found in salvage yards or boutique tile shops. Recycled tiles will add character and a vintage look to your design.

Top tips: Tiles

➢ *Ensure all tile adhesive and grout is healthy and humane (does not contain chemicals, which could release gases into the environment over time).*

➢ *Buy enough tiles to account for any breakages when laying the flooring.*

➢ *Identity what has been used to colour/glaze the tiles. Is it chemical free?*

➢ *Think about the lifecycle of the tiles. Can you source them locally (are they made in your country to reduce their shipping footprint?) and are they recyclable or biodegradable?*

Not all tiles are sustainable and humane. Some contain a synthetic plastic polymer called polyvinyl chloride, which in turn contains chemicals that can leak out over time, affecting the internal air quality. Make sure your tiles are made only from a clay mix and eco-friendly glaze, where at all possible.

Suppliers

Bert & May (reclaimed tiles)

Located in the United Kingdom.

Available worldwide.

Fireclay (tiles made from recycled materials)

Located in the United States.

Available worldwide.

Figure 4.9
Image provided by Fireclay
Pink Floor tile, features Fireclay's Picket tiles in Desert Bloom
Design and image: Sam Ushiro

Iris Ceramica

Located in Italy.

Available worldwide.

Figure 5.0
Image provided by Iris Ceramica

Maitland and Poate

Located in the United Kingdom.

Available worldwide.

Figure 5.1
Image provided by Maitland and Poate
www.maitlandandpoate.com
Photographer: Malcolm Menzies

Carpets and rugs

We all love that soft feeling underfoot. However, traditionally, carpets have been made from wool, silk or synthetic fibres (nylon, polypropylene or polyester, which are all derived from petroleum), making them a not particularly animal- and planet-friendly choice. In addition, traditional carpet designs use artificial dyes in the manufacture process, and the adhesives used for backing the carpets and the stain-repellents applied to their surface contain VOCs such as formaldehyde and other toxins. These substances release gases into the environment, having a negative effect on the internal air quality of a space.

Sustainable and humane carpets, on the other hand, consist of natural or recycled materials. This can include recycled plastic bottles, old carpets and disused fishing nets (found at the bottom of our oceans). Products used for attaching the backings onto the carpet comprise natural non-toxic adhesives. Eco-friendly and animal-friendly underlays are available, for instance Breathe, a natural product made from wood fibres. Carpets can help insulate a space, reducing your property's energy consumption. They're great in the design of hotels, especially if the property is an old castle or manor house.

Natural woven carpets and rugs

Made from plant fibres, including jute, sisal, seagrass, hemp and coir. The surface texture of natural fibre carpets can vary from soft to rough. They are suitable for areas of high traffic, but are not advised in areas of increased humidity such as bathrooms. They are available in a number of different colours, depending on the product. Natural woven carpets add texture and warmth, and have a calming effect on an interior design. The carpets would complement a variety of design styles, including modern, colonial or contemporary. Natural woven carpets are available in most countries: check online for your nearest supplier.

Organic cotton and recycled cotton rugs

Perhaps you want to add an ethnic or bohemian style to your design scheme? Organic and recycled cotton rugs are a great option for this. Recycled cotton rugs are made from discarded cotton clothing, whereas organic cotton rugs are made from 100% organic cotton. Both types of rugs are available in several different colours and styles; just be sure to check that any dyes are humane and healthy. To ensure the product is 100% organic cotton, look to see if the product is Global Organic Textile Standard (GOTS) certified. This is a worldwide recognized standard, which ensures the product is of 'organic status textile'. This ensures the product is both socially and responsibly made, from harvesting to finished item. Rugs can add an injection of colour, absorb unwanted noise and soften a design. Check online for your nearest supplier.

Banana silk carpet

A natural product made from the wood pulp of the banana plant. Banana silk carpets are 100% eco-friendly and are biodegradable, depending on the dyes, backings and adhesives that have been used in its manufacturing. It has a soft and velvety texture. Banana silk carpet adds glamour, style and luxury to any design, and is available in different colours. The carpet can be purchased from a number of bespoke carpet suppliers globally.

Recycled waste material

If purchasing a carpet made from recycled materials, check that it is not made from wool or silk as this would not be animal friendly. Carpets made from recycled materials feel soft. They're available in an array of different colours, complementing bold and bright interiors to calm and zen designs. Don't forget to ask what dyes have been used in manufacturing the carpets. Available from selected suppliers globally.

Top tips: Carpet

➢ *What area do you need the carpet for? Think about the volume of traffic within the space.*

➢ *What is the carpet made of?*

➢ *What ingredient has been used for the dye?*

➢ *What material has been used for backing the carpet?*

➢ *What adhesives have been used? Look for natural and non-toxic adhesives. Other adhesives may contain VOCs and toxins.*

➢ *Is the carpet responsibly manufactured?*

➢ *Is the carpet recyclable or biodegradable?*

Suppliers

Sisal and Seagrass

Located in the United Kingdom.

Available worldwide.

Figure 5.2
Sisal Boucle Carpet
Image provided by Sisal and Seagrass
Photographer: Mark Scott
Stylist: Charlie Davis

Figure 5.3
Sisal Babylon
Image provided by Sisal and Seagrass
Photographer: Mark Scott
Stylist: Charlie Davis

Figure 5.4
Sisal Babylon Grey
Image provided by Sisal and Seagrass
Photographer: Mark Scott
Stylist: Charlie Davis

Cork

Cork has been used as a flooring within interiors since at least 1904. As we saw from Part One, cork is a natural product, creating healthy and humane spaces. If you like a soft feeling underfoot, cork flooring could work for you. It contains no toxins, is water resistant and can help insulate your home. However, if you choose coloured cork flooring, be sure to check with the supplier what has been used to create the hues. Although cork flooring is a durable product, it can be easily marked if furniture is dragged along its surface. It is also not ideal for areas which are susceptible to high levels of moisture, for instance bathrooms and laundry rooms. It will help with the absorption of unwanted noise, add texture, and complement a number of different design styles.

Top tips: Cork

➤ *Is cork flooring suitable for the space you are designing?*

➤ *Check what pigments have been used to create the coloured cork flooring.*

➤ *On installation, ensure a healthy and humane certified adhesive is used.*

➤ *Buy enough cork tiles to account for cutting and damage when laying the flooring.*

Suppliers

Contact a local sustainably certified cork flooring specialist.

Natural linoleum

Linoleum is made from natural materials including linseed, ground cork dust, wood flour, rosin, limestone and eco-friendly pigments. If you like a soft feeling underfoot, linoleum can help you achieve this. Be aware that vinyl is not the same as natural linoleum. Vinyl is made from polyvinyl chloride (PVC), with the majority of it comprising petroleum, a non-sustainable material. Natural linoleum, on the other hand, is considered by some to be one of the most eco-friendly products available for flooring today. Linoleum has a positive lifecycle from extraction, comprising natural materials, to its end of life, where it is biodegradable. Linoleum flooring has a low level of natural VOCs.

Linoleum is available in an array of different colours, patterns and styles, adding contrast, colour and style to your design. Linoleum is water resistant and easy to clean, and is durable and versatile. However, it is not suitable flooring if you have pets as it will scratch. If well maintained, it can last for many years. Linoleum is available from a range of worldwide flooring suppliers.

Top tips: Linoleum flooring

➤ *Think sustainability: buy from a local eco-friendly certified stockist.*

➤ *If in any doubt about what the flooring is made from, contact the manufacturer directly.*

➤ *Ensure a healthy, non-toxic, chemical-free eco-friendly certified floor adhesive is used for laying the natural linoleum flooring.*

➤ *Don't forget that vinyl flooring is not the same as natural linoleum.*

➤ *Buy enough flooring to account for any unforeseen difficulties when laying the flooring.*

Suppliers

Contact a local sustainably certified natural linoleum flooring specialist.

Mogu Floor – Mycelium-based resilient flooring tiles

Mogu has also employed mushrooms' mycelium to create solutions for resilient flooring applications. Mogu Floor tiles are composed by, as cited by Mogu (2021), 'a 100% natural and biodegradable mycelium composite core-board, coupled with a proprietary bio-based resin characterized by a very high biological content (80%+ bio-based), resulting in final products whose effective bio-based composition is on average 90%+'.

Mogu Floor tiles are available in different textures, also depending on the choice of the organic (low-value) fillers utilized for each model, and they are characterized by a 'soft touch and matte finish'. The resilient flooring tiles can complement a number of different design styles, from classic to contemporary ones, and they have been designed taking into great consideration their entire lifecycle, as in fact at the end of their use the two main constituent parts (core + top layer) can be separated and individually upcycled to be embedded in new products.

Top tips: Mushroom (mycelium-based) resilient flooring tiles

➤ *Will it work with the space you are designing?*

➤ *Contact Mogu directly for the mycelium-based flooring tiles.*

Supplier

Mogu

Located in Italy.

Available worldwide.

Figure 5.5
Image provided by Mogu

Foresso flooring

Foresso layer flooring is made from 65% recycled content sourced from offcuts, wood waste from timber merchants or sawmills, and plaster waste from foundaries. The binder they use consists of wood dust, planing waste, mineral powders and 0% bio-based epoxy resin. Foresso (2021) states that 'the carbon footprint of this resin is approximately 40% lower than the equivalent petroleum-based product'. The resin used in Foresso flooring includes the 'latest innovations of bio-based chemistry (whose structure)… comprises plant origins'. Therefore, Foresso flooring's health and environmental benefits are greater than many whose flooring includes traditional resins. The plywood used to make this flooring is 100% FSC BB/BB Birch Throughout Plywood, selected because it does not contain the toxic glues used in other types of plywood. The flooring is finished in hardwax oil, which comprises natural oils and waxes.

Foresso flooring is sustainable throughout its lifecycle. The flooring contains no animal products. All materials can be reused at the end of its life. It is available in a number of different colours, which can add intrigue and contrast to a design. What also makes this product unique is that it can be used to make table and worktops. The flooring is suitable for both residential and commercial spaces; however, for commercial areas, the flooring needs to be finished in a commercial-based lacquer.

Top tips: Foresso flooring

➢ *Will it work with the space you are designing?*

➢ *Contact Foresso directly for the floor covering.*

➢ *Ensure any adhesives used are healthy, humane and eco-friendly certified.*

Supplier

Foresso

Located in the United Kingdom.

Available worldwide.

Figure 5.6
Image provided by Foresso

Figure 5.7
Image provided by Foresso

Figure 5.8
Image provided by Foresso

Figure 5.9
Image provided by Foresso

Part Three
Furniture

From feature pieces to hidden-away treasures, furniture is generally chosen due to its specific function required within a space. Flatpack furniture has become a popular choice when furnishing our homes and work spaces: this revolution has enabled people to keep up with the modern way of life. Jobs these days can require people to move around, both nationally and internationally. Do you take the furniture with you; if it is from Ikea, do you return it to one of its new-style stores, or do you dispose of it (sell or throw it away) and start all over again? Sometimes cost can be the determining factor. In addition to the desire to keep up with ever-changing interior design trends, we need to ask ourselves: are we actually creating positive spaces, which promote our health and wellbeing? In the United Kingdom alone, 22 million pieces of furniture are thrown away every year (Nicholson, 2018). Are the choices you are making to furnish your home and office really creating healthy, positive and mindful spaces?

Good furniture placement can promote a positive flow of energy throughout your home. It's important not to overdo it: too many pieces in a space can start to look and feel overcrowded, creating stress and making the room look like an assault course. When considering the placement of furniture, it may be worth using the principles of Feng Shui, an ancient Chinese art born more than 3000 years ago. Feng Shui involves designing your home to facilitate positive energy, in order to promote harmony and a balanced life. If Feng Shui is not your thing, then maybe the practice of zoning will work for you? This is where you create 'zones' within your home, which represent where one space ends and another one begins. For instance, if you have an open-plan space comprising kitchen, dining and lounge area, you could place the back of the sofa to the dining area to signal where the dining room starts and the lounge ends.

Add some fun to your design: why not mix up the styles of seating? Instead of including two matching sofas in your sitting room or waiting area, you could shop around and include seating of different forms. This will add intrigue and is a good option if your design style is of a vintage/retro theme. If you like a more conservative and balanced approach, reflect what one side of the room looks like to the opposite side (mirror it).

This part of the book is organized a little differently. Because there are so many different types of furniture, instead of taking you through all these different types, we're going to look instead at the different factors to consider when choosing furniture for your space. These factors will apply to pretty much every piece you need, allowing you to make informed choices, whatever your furniture needs. The chapters in Part Three cover: the basic materials used in furniture production; what makes an item of furniture sustainable and animal friendly; alternative approaches to buying furniture; examples of sustainable and animal-friendly furniture; top tips and sustainable furniture suppliers.

Basic materials used in furniture production

There are a number of different types of materials used to create furniture, not all of which promote sustainability or are animal friendly. Below is a list of materials commonly used within furniture products.

Plain wood

Ensure all wood included within the furniture is FSC certified. Recycled wood is now being used by some furniture makers, which is a great alternative to using new wood.

Metal

There are many different metals, but probably the most common in furniture manufacture is steel. Steel is recognized as being a sustainable product because it can be recycled and re-used. Steel is used in different types of furniture, from tables to beds. However, the finish of the steel may not be considered healthy. Always double check what finishes have been used and what they are made from.

Plywood

Plywood is wood made by gluing together thin sheets of wood. The thin sheets of wood can be softwood or hardwood. This type of wood is also known as veneer. The adhesives used for gluing the wood together can sometimes contain unhealthy substances such as formaldehyde; always check what glues have been used if this is a material of your choice.

Particle board (chipboard)

Used a lot in the manufacturing of furniture, particle board is made from the waste of wood manufacturing, for instance sawdust. It is made by all the waste materials being glued and squashed together through a heat process. However, due to the adhesives containing chemicals and the plastic coating used to finish off the particle board, it is not recyclable or biodegradable. Furthermore, it can have a negative effect on our internal air quality due to the VOCs included.

Upholstery fabric

There are a huge range of fabrics used in the upholstering of furniture: leather alternatives, silk, velvet, nylon, polyester, cotton, linen or wool – just to start with. The choice of fabric can be influenced by what the furniture is going to be used for. However, not all of these fabrics are animal friendly and sustainable. Nylon, for example, is made from petroleum. It is not biodegradable and can contain chemicals. Polyester is another man-made fabric made from polymers which contains chemicals. However, there are now a number of alternative eco-friendly and animal-friendly alternatives, including plant-based alternatives for leather, which will be discussed in Part Five.

Upholstery filling/mattresses

Traditionally, some upholstery filling and mattresses are made from polyurethane foam. This is a man-made product and can contain VOCs. Other fillers include memory foam, which is used in mattresses and can contain formaldehyde, benzene and naphthalene (Savvy Rest, 2020).

Down, hollow fibre, cotton, wool wadding and polyester are other types of fillings used. Down and wool wadding are sustainable, but not animal friendly. Polyester is a synthetic fibre made from petroleum, which can be non-recyclable or biodegradable.

Plastic

Everyone knows about the effects of plastic on the planet, especially in our oceans. However, some plastic can be recyclable at the end of its life. Furniture made from recycled plastic is sustainable as the material has been re-used – so much better than ending up in landfill or the ocean. Bear in mind, though, that this isn't a perfect solution: once the plastic has been re-used to make an item, can it be recycled again at the end of its second life? Also, the energy costs of recycling plastic furniture into new items of furniture can be quite high. However, recycled plastic chairs are becoming more readily available now, and it may well be the most appropriate solution for you.

Rattan (wicker furniture)

Rattan is a vine, part of the palm family, which is grown in Asia. It can be used in interior and exterior furniture. The vine is harvested, its stems are dried, stored for a period of time and then woven into furniture. Rattan is a sustainable and animal-friendly product.

Bamboo

As we know, bamboo is a sustainable and animal-friendly product. Bamboo can be used to create the frame for chairs, beds, bedside tables, mirrors and the head of a bed. It is biodegradable, depending upon the finish, if any, which has been applied to the bamboo. The knot chair is one example of bamboo furniture, made entirely from eco-friendly bamboo.

Paint and varnish (lacquer) finishes

Traditional wood and metal paints or lacquers can contain chemicals and heavy metals, for instance formaldehyde, which is harmful to the environment. Eco-friendly paints and lacquers are plant and water-based products. However, as identified in Part One, these may not be animal friendly. Always check with the furniture manufacturer to identify what paint/finish has been used to cover the furniture.

Fire retardants, stain-resistant treatments and wrinkle-resistant treatments

Flame retardants are chemicals that are applied to materials to prevent the start, or slow the growth of, fire (National Institute of Environmental Health, 2020). These are sometimes required by commercial standards, and can help to make an otherwise flammable item of furniture safe. For stain resistant treatments, the chemical typically used is perfluorochemicals (PFCs). Wrinkle-resistant treatments prevent the item of furniture from becoming wrinkled and can comprise chemicals, for instance formaldehyde. Fire retardants, stain and wrinkle resistances are considered to be toxic due to being made from several different chemicals.

Figure 6.0
Sage Table in European oak
Image provided by Konk Furniture, a company located in the United Kingdom. Products only available in the United Kingdom.
Photographer and stylist: Beth Kaye

Figure 6.1
Chamfered Edge Cabinet in black American walnut
Image provided by Konk Furniture, a company located in the United Kingdom. Products only available in the United Kingdom.
Photographer and stylist: Beth Kaye

What makes an item of furniture sustainable and animal friendly?

How can you identify whether or not an item of furniture is sustainable and animal friendly? In determining this, you have to consider a number of different factors – some of which we have considered already in the flooring and wall covering sections.

Materials and manufacturing process

Just like for everything you source, you will want to identify all of the materials used in creating your furniture piece – from their extraction at source to those used in the manufacturing process. Sustainable furniture may comprise products which have been recycled from consumer rubbish. For instance, recycled plastic can be used to create carpets.

Products made from fast-growing materials, for instance rattan or bamboo, are highly sustainable – in fact, not only is bamboo able to grow fast but it can absorb large amounts of carbon dioxide (CO_2). Cork, identified in Part One, is a great sustainable and animal-friendly option due to the way the product is harvested and manufactured. Look for FSC certified wooden furniture, or furniture which contains recycled wood.

What adhesives have been used to manufacture the furniture? Do they contain any unwanted chemicals? To identify this, you may need to contact the manufacturer directly. Fire retardants are still a legal requirement in some countries for both residential and commercial properties. However, Cottonsafe® Natural Mattress in the United Kingdom have created animal-friendly and chemical-free mattresses. Be aware that some products advertised as natural may contain wool or other animal by-products, making them sustainable but not animal friendly.

Upholstery filling

New sustainable options include products such as coir (coconut husks), which is biodegradable. Cotton batting is upholstery filling made from layers of 100% cotton. Natural latex is a good option, but is not advisable for people with a latex allergy. Latex is collected from rubber trees and is biodegradable. In addition, latex is resilient to dust mites, mould and mildew. These are just some of the great alternatives to traditional foam-filled upholstery.

Upholstery coverings

Sustainable and animal-friendly furniture coverings include linen, hemp, 100% (GOTS certified) organic cotton and alternative leather (made from plant-based alternatives, for instance banana leaf and apple ten lork, and cactus). Avoid velvet made from synthetic fibres: these can contain chemicals, again causing off-gassing into your home. Any fabric which is plant based does not contain harmful chemicals and has ethical manufacturing processes.

Ethical manufacturing processes

One of the most important ethical manufacturing processes to look out for is Fair Trade. This means that people making products in developing countries are paid a respectable amount for the manufacturing of an item, protecting them from exploitation. The working conditions of staff employed are humane and not detrimental to their health or the surrounding communities. In addition, the methods used in manufacturing are not detrimental to the environment (rivers or land) and produce little or no carbon emissions. Finally, the sourcing of the materials should not strip the natural environment of this material. Look for Fair Trade and other similar certifications to ensure the furniture uses ethical manufacturing processes.

Transportation/logistics

Can you buy this product locally? Do you need to purchase it from overseas? Purchasing products from overseas can increase the carbon footprint of a product, having a negative effect on the lifecycle of a product. Buy local as much as possible. When purchasing a product, identify where it is actually made: you may be surprised to find out that it is not made where you think it is.

Is it functional for your needs?

Does the furniture fulfil your requirements? For instance, is it multifunctional? A sofa bed which is a sofa during the day and a bed by night will reduce the need for multiple pieces of furniture, and reduce your overall impact. Is the sofa durable, and will it survive any children or pets? Do you really need it? Will it block the flow of traffic through a space or make a room look cluttered? An important principle of humane and sustainable design is to choose the items that fit your needs and no more – this keeps the carbon footprint smaller, creates a more positive space that allows movement and reduces future waste.

Cheap versus expensive

When it comes to buying furniture, two of the big influences on our choices are cost and practicality. Money is often even more of an influence when it comes to design projects for the workplace. Flatpack furniture has become a new way of furnishing our homes and offices for a lower cost. However, although cheap and convenient, a lot of this furniture is made with particle board and covered in a laminate or veneer finish. Not only is particle board usually unsustainable, but if the item of furniture made from particle board becomes spoiled, it cannot be restored, meaning the life of the product is shorter than it otherwise could have been. A lot of cheap furniture can be made in countries where the working practices may not be of the highest standard. Think about how, where and what the furniture is made of, and whether it can be re-used at the end of its life.

If opting for more expensive furniture, shop around. In doing so, you may find the same item of furniture is cheaper with another supplier. This will then allow more of your budget to be used elsewhere in the design of a space. If your budget is limited, identify what is in the product, where it was made and if it is sustainable (recyclable or biodegradable) and animal friendly. If it is not sustainable, could you save and purchase a more expensive article at a later date?

Alternatively, you may not need to purchase new furniture at all. What can you move around your home or office space to make it look more appealing? What do you have stored away in a store cupboard or garage? If you are part of a hotel chain, can this be used within another property? For the home, if you don't have the funds to buy the more expensive item of furniture, why not temporarily fill the space with second-hand furniture? This is a great sustainable method, and items can be given away or re-sold when no longer required. Consider buying antique furniture if it suits your design. Buying cheap doesn't always mean it will last. Less is not always best.

Made to order, not mass produced

Mass-produced furniture often uses materials which can be detrimental to the environment, creating a negative effect on our internal air quality. Made-to-order furniture, however, can be much more expensive. This could well be a case of getting what you pay for, though, as bespoke furniture is often a more sustainable and animal-friendly alternative. You can choose what materials you want the furniture to be made from and finished off in, meaning it fits your space perfectly and you can choose the materials you want in order to keep it sustainable and animal friendly. Furniture which has been bespoke made is more likely to not be changed, but handed down the family – meaning the life of the product is longer.

The availability of sustainable furniture is increasing, including Vadim Kibardin's new range of furniture made from paper. In addition, architect, designer and creative director José Manuel Carvalho Araújo has created a unique range from cork. Other types of sustainable furniture now available can comprise waste from industrial waste in lumbar factories. In addition, the Ottan Studio have created a coffee table made from old lentils and grass trimmings. The table also comes with a lamp, which is made from carrot pulp, orange peel and artichoke leaves.

Alternative approaches to buying furniture

In the previous chapter, we touched on the idea of alternatives to buying new furniture for your space. There are several different alternative methods for furnishing your home which are recognized as being sustainable and animal friendly; here are three possible alternative approaches for furnishing your home.

For hire

Select companies are now offering a service whereby you can hire furniture for an agreed length of time. This service in the interior design industry follows that of the clothing industry, and could well be a great way to refresh the design of a space with the latest style. Once finished with, or no longer required, the furniture is returned to the company rather than ending up in a landfill somewhere. Check online for companies who provide this service.

Second-hand furniture/antiques

There are a lot of companies now offering a great selection of second-hand furniture. Shopping for second-hand furniture can be a fun experience; attending house clearances, car boot sales, flea markets and re-cycling centres are some interesting places to find second-hand furniture. You never know what you can pick up! If you're looking for that ultimate piece of furniture for your space, check out antique shops or local small auction houses – a quality antique piece, whilst technically being second hand, can add real luxury and grandeur to a space. Another great thing about buying second-hand furniture is it can reduce the amount of off-gassing in your home due to it not being new and straight from the manufacturer.

Repurpose your old furniture

Ask yourself: can I transform the item of furniture so it complements the new design? This can be in your home or place of business. For instance, re-paint the furniture another colour or change the upholstery fabric. When upscaling an item of furniture, proceed with care when stripping any paints/finishes as they could contain toxic substances. Make sure you have the appropriate protective clothing on: for instance, a face mask. The great thing about revamping furniture is it will match the other objects in the space because you can finish it in matching textures or colours. Therefore, it makes your design flow and be aesthetically pleasing to the eye.

Top tips: Furniture

➢ *Does it fit? Will it allow for the free flow of traffic around the space?*

➢ *Does the colour complement the design of the space? Does it create a positive vibe, promoting your health and wellbeing?*

➢ *What is the furniture's lifecycle? What is it made from? What are the processes used in its manufacturing? Has it been covered in chemicals? Where is it made (is this ethical, what about the carbon footprint)? Is it recyclable or biodegradable?*

➢ *Look for seat cushions made from natural latex foam or other humane and sustainable materials.*

➢ *If restoring old pieces of furniture, be careful when removing any old paint or varnishes as these may contain toxins.*

➢ *When re-painting, varnishing or lacquering furniture, identify what materials are used to make the product. This should be labelled on the tin; if not, contact the supplier.*

➢ *What is it finished with?*

➢ *When you buy furniture, think of it as an investment. Spending more money today will save you money in the long run.*

➢ *Do you need to change the furniture?*

➢ *Is the furniture animal friendly?*

➢ *Does it fulfil the purpose you need it for?*

➢ *Buying second-hand furniture not only is a sustainable option, but could help to reduce the off-gassing of furniture in your house.*

➢ *Buy furniture which is sustainably certified. Don't forget: if it is advertised as being natural or organic but is not certified it may be greenwashing.*

Suppliers

Bolia

Located in Denmark.

Contact the company for availability.

José Manuel Carvalho Araújo

Located in both Brazil and Portugal.

Contact the company for availability.

Konk Furniture

Located in the United Kingdom.

Available in the United Kingdom only.

Mater Design

Located in Denmark.

Contact the company for availability.

Norm Architect

Located in Denmark.

Contact the company for availability.

Ottan Studio

Located in Turkey.

Contact the company for availability.

Sebastian Cox

Located in the United Kingdom.

Contact the company for availability.

Tom Raffield

Located in the United Kingdom.

Available worldwide.

Figure 6.2
Arbor Armchair
Image provided by Tom Raffield

Figure 6.3
May Coffee Table
Image provided by Tom Raffield

Part Four
Lighting

Lighting – whether artificial light like lamps, overhead lights or candles, or natural daylight – is incredibly important in interior design. Not only is it needed to light a space (of course!), but it can also create the proposed ambience for a space and illuminate key features within a design. When we think about lighting design, there are three elements to consider: brightness, saturation and hue. Brightness refers to the amount of light emitted, saturation is the intensity of the colour of the light, and hue is the colour of a light.

As with all your design elements, when considering light, it's important to know what the space will be used for. For instance, in a dining area within a restaurant or home, you would not want a brightly lit space: this would not create a calm and relaxing ambience for eating. Instead, a softly lit space is recommended. Or, if a space has a dual purpose, you may want to use dimmer switches to allow for flexibility.

One great technique used to create a balanced lighting design is called layered lighting. Layered lighting is when you combine different types of lighting: for instance, a chandelier, some table lamps and some floor lamps. With this selection, you would have a ceiling-level light (chandelier), mid-level light (floor lamp) and low-level light (table lamp). Here's another example: a bathroom lighting design could include a ceiling light, natural daylight from a window, recessed, low-level light-emitting diode (LED) wall lights inside the shower area, and candles strategically placed around the bathroom.

Part Four will look at: the effects of lighting on our wellbeing; environmental effects of lighting; traditional methods of lighting; sustainable methods of lighting; light fittings; and examples of sustainable and animal-friendly light fittings. Like Part Three on furniture, the top tips and list of possible suppliers will be gathered at the end of the section, rather than spread throughout.

Effects of lighting on our wellbeing

How a space is lit can affect us both mentally and physically. For instance, lighting can affect our levels of concentration, appetite, and mood (TCPI, 2020). Light can be either warm or cool: warm light makes a room feel warm, peaceful and cosy. A warmly lit space usually has quite a low level of light and creates a space to chill out and unwind. On the other hand, a space lit by bright, cool lighting can stimulate your senses, making you feel more alert and energized. This stimulation of our senses can also increase the intensity of our emotions, which could have a positive or a negative effect on your wellbeing. Therefore, spaces lit with low-level lighting can help you maintain your emotions at a more reasonable level, whilst further enabling you to make more logical decisions. Additionally, light can affect our perception of things and how we sleep.

The colour of light can have an effect on our emotions and how we perceive things. For instance, a red light can create a sense of warmth and love. However, as TCPI (2020) cites, (red) lighting can also result in a sense of 'danger'. Green light, on the other hand, can create a feeling of harmony with nature, calming and enhancing our wellbeing. Blue, as cited by TCPI (2020), can 'promote wisdom' and exudes luxury. Orange lighting emanates warmth and vitality and white light promotes cleanliness.

Environmental effects of lighting

How we light our home and work affects the amount of energy we consume. It is considered that in the majority of our homes, lighting accounts for 15% of our energy bill. For those of you who work in a commercial environment, lighting accounts for 25% of the energy bill. It is recognized that lighting is responsible for about one-sixth to one-fifth of the world's electricity consumption. It's not just about the light bulb you use, though, but your light fitting too. As with furniture, flooring and wall coverings, it's important to consider the materials and processes used in making the lamps and light fittings themselves. If you are able, look for light fittings that have been made from sustainable materials. If unsure, contact the supplier directly for information on what the light fittings are made from.

Here are a few tips on how you could decrease your lighting energy consumption:

> *Turn off lights in all spaces not being used.*

> *Include dimmer switches in a space. This will dull the light, creating the desired ambience, especially in the evenings, therefore decreasing your energy requirements and costs.*

> *Use motion sensors, which activate the lights to come on when entering a space.*

> *Utilize as much natural daylight as possible within a space – keep curtains and blinds open, and try not to block the light from a window with furniture.*

Types of lighting

Here are a few different types of lighting that you may want to consider including in your layered lighting design.

Light bulbs: Candescent and light-emitting diode (LED)

Traditional methods of lighting include the use of candescent light bulbs. These are made from a glass outer case with a tungsten filament (a piece of wire) coiled inside. When an electrical current passes through the filament, it creates both light and heat. The amount of energy required to produce light in these bulbs is very high, and they are not very efficient as much of the energy used is lost in the form of unneeded or unwanted heat. This is why the newer lower energy requirement bulbs were introduced, and why candescent bulbs are no longer available in some countries.

LEDs, in contrast, are bulbs which create light by the flow of electricity through a diode (an electronic component) instead of a filament. They work on a similar principle to that of candescent bulbs but are considered to be greatly energy efficient, lasting around 100 times longer than traditional light bulbs. They produce less heat, their power needs are lower and they are more durable as well. Not only will LED light bulbs cost you less in terms of energy consumption but they also do not contain toxic elements, which means they can be disposed of more easily and safely. LED lighting is more versatile too in that it can be used to illuminate specific areas within a space, whereas traditional light bulbs illuminate in every direction, whether you want them to or not. LED lighting can be controlled by smart lighting systems, which can further reduce the energy consumption of your home and office.

Daylighting

When designing a space, one particularly sustainable approach is to maximize the amount of natural light entering it. This will decrease your energy costs and consumption. Spaces that optimize as much daylight as possible promote a much calmer, more serene and more welcoming space, enhancing people's mental and physical wellbeing. This can be achieved by including the following: windows, skylights, sunlight transportation systems, light tubes/tunnels, translucent panels and atriums.

Windows and skylights

Windows are good for both light and ventilation. A skylight is a window situated within the roof of your office or home; although these can cause elevated temperatures within a space in the summer, there are different types of glazing available that can reduce this problem.

Sunlight transportation systems

A sunlight transportation system is a relatively new method, wherein sunlight is caught by roof panels and then transferred along optic cables up to 15 metres long and diffused into the proposed space. As with all lighting designs, this can be used as part of a layered lighting design and is a potentially fantastic solution for spaces that do not have many windows or other means of accessing daylight.

Light tubes/tunnels

Simply put, light tunnels are structures added to an interior's design to help promote daylighting. They can also be used to transfer artificial light to a space. Also known as sun pipes, they work sort of like a backwards telescope, reflecting light down a cylinder to move it into a space that otherwise would not get light from windows.

Translucent panels

Translucent panels are light glazing panels which are sandwiched together. The panels allow natural light to pass through. They can be used in office blocks, hospitals, warehouses and more. They're essentially windows, but are not for ventilation (as they don't open) and can be better in terms of safety standards.

Atriums

Atriums are basically one big roof skylight, surrounded by a building. Atriums were commonly included in, and considered to be a key feature of, Roman building design. Atriums (or atria, if we're going to be technical about it!) light up a space with lots of natural daylight, as they are able to capture light wherever the sun is, unlike a smaller skylight which may not get much light at certain times of day. Examples of this include the Pantheon (Rome), which contains no glass and, more recently, the British Museum (London), which is covered in glass.

Light fittings

Look for light fittings which are made from natural or recycled materials. Like furniture, one source of recycled materials might be antiques: as long as you make sure it has been restored to a safe standard and comes with a guarantee, you might well be saving something beautiful from going into a landfill. If antique doesn't fit your aesthetic, you could look for materials such as recycled paper, glass, metal, plastic or natural materials like wood, felt and cloth. What about lamps made from recycled bottles and jars? Bicycle Glass, a company based in the United States, makes pendant lights from 100% recycled glass. Check out their website in the glossary at the back of this book. This could also be an option.

You can set the mood of each space by the brightness and colour of the lighting you include. So, when buying lamps, there are two main things to consider: brightness and colour.

The brightness of traditional-style lamps is measured in watts: the higher the wattage, the brighter the lamp. For LED lamps, the brightness is measured in lumens: the higher the lumen, the brighter the lamp.

The Kelvin rating identifies the colour of a light and is stated on the lamp packaging. For example and as cited by Martin (2018), the Kelvin rating comprises four temperature categories: 'soft light (2700–3000 Kelvin); warm light (3000–4000 Kelvin); bright light (4000–5000 Kelvin); and daylight (5000–6500 Kelvin)'.

In a work space, light colours should generally fall into the bright and daylight categories. In a dining room, 'warm light' is recommended. If your dining area is used for other tasks, I recommend you include a dimmer switch to alter the brightness of the light according to your activities (eating, reading, etc.).

Have you ever wondered what some of the lettering on a lamp refers to? This can indicate the shape and size of the lamp. For instance, the letter 'A' stands for standard lamp; this can also be referred to as 'E', for an 'Edison' lamp. The letter 'B' stands for a 'blunt end' lamp: simply put, a candle-shaped lamp. 'G' stands for a 'globs' lamp, and 'BR' refers to 'bulging reflector' lamp. These are a few of the most popular types of lamps available.

Top tips: Lighting

➤ *Buy lighting from a reputable (sustainable) lighting supplier. If in doubt, check with the manufacturer.*

➤ *Identify the energy consumption of the light fitting.*

➤ *Identify what the light fitting is made from, including finishes.*

➤ *What about considering an open-plan home or office space to help light reach more easily throughout the space?*

➤ *When decorating a space, consider the colour of paint you are choosing. Why? Dark paints create a darker-looking space, which will absorb a lot of the light. However, light hues will reflect light around a space, creating a more energy-efficient space.*

➤ *Use floor lamps, wall lamps or table lamps to light a part of a space. This will save you from having to light the whole space, reducing your energy consumption and needs.*

➤ *When wanting to change the ambience of a space, use dimmers. This is particularly good in spaces such as dining rooms, bedrooms (especially infant nurseries and children's rooms) or bathrooms.*

➤ *Consider light-washing the walls – this means illuminating your walls, which will bounce light around the space.*

➤ *Implement a layered lighting design.*

➤ *Use LED light bulbs but ensure the ones you select will not have an impact on the environment at the end of their life.*

➤ *Include as much natural daylight as possible, through windows, daylight delivery systems, skylights or light tunnels.*

➤ *Include smart lighting sensor systems.*

➤ *Choose appropriate light fittings.*

➤ *Put light where it is needed.*

Suppliers

Asano Japanese lighting

Located in Japan.

Available worldwide from a selection of stockists.

AY Illuminate

Sustainable lighting made from a range of products, including bamboo, rattan, recycled cartons, hand-made paper and aluminium. AY Illuminate are located in the Netherlands.

Contact supplier for availability.

Figure 6.4
Image supplied by AY Illuminate

Figure 6.5
Twiggy Egg Pendant
Copyright DESIREE at Euromobil

Figure 6.6
Rattan Bell
Copyright Spence and Lynda
Australian Distributors for AY Illuminate

Cerno

A sustainable and animal-friendly lighting company based in California. They say their design style is 'an intersection of modernism and contemporary design'.

Available in the United States, France, Canada and Mexico.

Figure 6.7
Image provided by Cerno

Figure 6.8
Image provided by Cerno

David Trubridge

Located in New Zealand.

Available worldwide; check with supplier.

Graypants

Located in Amsterdam and Seattle (United States).

Available worldwide; check with supplier.

Norm Architect

Located in Denmark.

Contact supplier for availability.

Octó Candles

Located in the United Kingdom.

Candles made from soy wax, containing 100% natural ingredients. Octó candles are made by all materials being hand blended. The candles include a cotton wick. Octó Candles (2020) says: 'all products are animal friendly and contain no synthetic or chemical nasties'.

Available worldwide; check with supplier.

Figure 6.9

Figure 7.0

Images provided by Octó Candles

Figure 7.1
Image provided by Octó Candles

Recycled/antique chandeliers

(Available from a reputable supplier or antique store.)

Slamp

An Italian bespoke lighting company located just outside Rome. In 2020, Slamp launched its new project focusing on 'planet wellbeing', by transforming leftover materials into portable beehives. They use long-lasting technopolymers in the production of their lights, materials which are recyclable and that 'reduce environmental costs four times more than other materials' (Slamp, 2021).

Contact supplier for further information.

Figure 7.2
Image provided by Ph. Pedro Sadio, courtesy of Slamp

Figure 7.3
Image provided by Ph. Pedro Sadio, courtesy of Slamp

Figure 7.4
Clizia Mama Non Mama by Adriano Rachele

Figure 7.5
Clizia Mama Non Mama by Adriano Rachele

Tom Raffield

Located in the United Kingdom.

Available worldwide.

WU lamp made of rice paper

(Available from a number of online retailers.)

Part Five
Fabric

What do you need to consider when buying fabric or upholstered products? Apart from the eternal consideration of budget, questions can include: will it complement the proposed design; will it make the space look too light or too dark; will it add warmth and help insulate the space in the cooler months but also make it feel cooler in the warmer months; and finally, will it withstand children and pets? Fabric can soften a design whilst adding an injection of colour. Additionally, it can add texture, depth and character. Then, of course, we have considerations of sustainability and animal friendliness.

The processes involved in manufacturing certain non-sustainable and non-animal-friendly fabrics may include products being bleached, treated with various alkali products to increase a fabric's strength and enhance its look, and the use of synthetic dyes. Synthetic dyes can contain VOCs, which as we know are undesirable for a healthy space, but natural dyes are available and can consist of plants, fruits, minerals and other sources. Some manufacturing practices require a lot of water and energy, and create a significant amount of waste, which is bad for the fabric's carbon footprint. Furthermore, some traditional methods for creating certain fabrics, for instance silk (made from the silkworm) and leather (made from cattle), are considered to be detrimental to both the environment and animals. However, new methods have been established for creating more humane alternatives to these types of fabrics.

Part Five will look at what makes a fabric sustainable and animal friendly and it will also examine sustainable and animal-friendly fabrics. As with Parts Three and Four the top tips and supplier list will be at the end instead of spread throughout.

What makes a fabric sustainable and animal friendly?

When shopping for fabric, online or in a store, there is an overwhelming selection of colours, textures and styles. However, like everything else, how the fabric has been made and the materials it has been made from will determine whether or not it is sustainable and animal friendly. The textile industry is changing, with new healthy and humane products becoming more readily available. So how can you identify whether or not a fabric is sustainable and animal friendly? Once again, it's about reviewing the lifecycle of the product you want to use: its raw material, how it is manufactured and its end of life (is it recyclable, reusable or biodegradable?). Was the fabric manufactured ethically, at no detriment to the communities who farm or make it? Does it require high volumes of water and energy to make? Some fabrics can use a number of different inorganic salts, pigments, heavy metals and chemicals in their manufacturing process whilst also generating large amounts of waste, which can result in an increase of emissions into the environment. Conversely, some fabric-making processes may comprise what is known as a 'closed circuit': a system whereby water is recycled time and time again and used for the production of the fabric.

One method for identifying whether fabrics such as cotton are sustainable is to look for the Global Organic Textile Standard (GOTS) certification:

The aim of the standard is to define world-wide recognized requirements that ensure organic status of textiles, from harvesting of the raw materials, through environmentally and socially responsible manufacturing up to the labelling in order to provide a credible assurance to the end consumer.

(GOTS, 2016)

Animal-friendly fabrics, in particular, might be plant-based alternatives which replace traditional fabrics like leather and wool. Don't forget though that even if the fabric is animal friendly, the processes used in manufacturing may not be sustainable – so it's always worth checking.

Sustainable and animal-friendly fabrics

L et's have a look at some of the fabric options out there that are friendlier to animals and our planet.

Leather alternatives

Gone are the days when leather-look fabric either had to be made from animal skin or polyvinyl chloride (a synthetic material made from polymer plastic). Today, there are a great range of alternatives, many of which are both animal friendly and sustainable. Here are a few.

Piñatex

An alternative to leather made from pineapple leaves, created by Dr Carmen Hijosa. Dr Hijosa wanted to create an alternative to leather that has less of an environmental impact and is humane. What was once just a culinary delight is now becoming an item to help furnish and decorate our homes and places of work. Piñatex has a positive lifecycle, and can be broken down or re-used when a product is finished with.

Cork

As we know, cork comes from the bark of a cork oak tree. The removal of the bark does not compromise the life or health of the tree as it is able to re-grow. Cork's natural composition creates a toxin-free and eco-friendly space. It has a positive lifecycle (extraction to end of life) due to being a natural and biodegradable product. It can last up to 50 years and promotes a clean, healthy and humane environment. Cork is most commonly used as an upholstery alternative to leather.

Linoleum

Developed by designer Don Yaw Kwaning, fabric linoleum includes natural plant-based oils. Kwaning has created two types: a thick material which can be used as a wall covering and a thinner alternative, which has a similar texture to the leather originally used to make a saddle bag. This alternative leather is used for upholstering furniture.

Figure 7.6
Image provided by Don Yaw Kwaning

Figure 7.7
Image provided by Don Yaw Kwaning

Mushrooms

This type of alternative to leather is made from mycelium. The fabric is breathable and water repellent. This alternative to leather is used in furniture production.

Palm

Created by Tjeerd Veenhoven, a designer from the Netherlands. The palm alternative to leather is made from the leaves of the areca palm, also known as the Betel tree. It is commonly grown in Asia. The material is used for the upholstering of furniture.

Apple ten lork

An alternative to leather, which is made from the waste of apple agroindustry.

Cassina used this upholstery for a selection of furniture in the installation 'Cassina Croque La Pomme' by Phillip Starck with the aim of exploring new forms of expression with alternative materials.

Fleather

A team of researchers from an Indian Institute of Technology Kanpur-backed biomaterial start-up company based in Haling, Kanpur, India, were working on projects regarding flower waste and its uses. After careful analysis of a pile of unused flowers, a dense fibrous mat was discovered. This dense fibrous mat texture resembled something similar to leather. From this discovery, a plant-based alternative to leather was developed, called Fleather. In 2019, this new type of alternative to leather was presented with the United Nations Sustainability award.

Cloth fabrics

Let's now look at some of the non-leather-alternative options, including wool alternatives, silk alternatives and plant-based cloth.

100% organic cotton

Organic cotton is cotton which has been farmed under a specific set of agricultural standards (About Organic Cotton.org, 2016). For instance, the methods used to produce the cotton are designed to sustain the health of the soil, ecosystems and people by using natural processes rather than artificial inputs – this means that the cotton is grown using no harmful chemicals. Check out the Organic Cotton.org website for the method used for growing organic cotton.

The method used in farming organic cotton uses 88% less water and requires 62% less energy than non-organic farming practices. In addition, because it uses no pesticides or insecticides, those who farm the cotton are in a safer work environment. Find out whether the cotton you are using is 100% organic by checking whether it is GOT certified, for natural fibres, or Oeko-Tex Standard 100 certified for plant-based synthetic fabrics such as cotton blends. Oeko-Tex thoroughly tests fabric, through every component, for harmful substances and certifies only those which have been shown to be harmless.

Jute

Jute is a shiny bast fibre which comes from the bark of the Corchorus capsularis (jute plant). It takes four months to grow and is grown in places such as Bangladesh and India. It is considered to be a sustainable material due to it requiring less water than, for instance, cotton. In addition, it is a biodegradable and recyclable product. Jute fibres are cut, grouped together and then soaked in water. The outer part of the fibre is then removed, leaving the soft fibres of jute to be taken out and processed. Jute can be used to make a wide range of products, including: curtains, rugs, carpets and furniture coverings such as headboards.

Hemp

When people think of hemp, they tend to think of marijuana. However, hemp that is used to make fabrics is not the same as marijuana; also known as industrial hemp, it contains no tetrahydrocannabinol (THC), which is the active ingredient in marijuana as a drug. Industrial hemp can grow quickly and with little water, and does not require the use of pesticides. Hemp is resilient to disease and can grow in small spaces, therefore helping to prevent deforestation. However, due to hemp being associated with marijuana, its supply is not as readily available as other products such as cotton or jute.

Organic linen

Linen is a fabric made from fibres of the flax plant. It's a breathable material which is stronger than cotton. The flax plant does not require the large volumes of water that is needed for growing cotton, and organic linen is grown without the use of pesticides, herbicides and fungicides, making it safer for the planet and for the farmers. It is biodegradable and animal friendly. However, its sustainability can be affected by the types of dyes that may be used in the manufacturing process, so try to ensure that any linen you choose is GOTS certified. It is a strong and durable fabric, ideal for bedlinen, upholstery fabric, curtains and blinds. It creates a sense of style whilst insulating a space in the winter and keeping it cool in the summer months.

Silk

Lotus silk

The lotus flower is recognized as a symbol of divine purity. Described by some as 'the Yarn from Buddha's Flower', lotus silk is made from the delicate fibres of the lotus flower stems. The lotus flower does not require the need for pesticides in its growth and needs only a minimal amount of water. There is little to no waste in the production of the silk and it typically originates from Myanmar and Cambodia. Lotus silk is woven on hand looms and is dyed using natural colour pigments. Just as durable as normal silk, it is biodegradable at the end of its life.

Citrus silk

Citrus silk is a silk made from the waste of the citrus industry. Cellulose collected from this waste is spun into a yarn and then turned into a silk fabric. The silk can be made completely of citrus waste or it can be mixed with other yarns. It is a biodegradable silk fabric.

Soy silk

Soy silk is not a new concept. In the 1940s, Japan explored the use of soy as an alternative to traditional silk-making processes. This was then further tested in the United States in 1945. Made from the waste created by the food production of soya, such as tofu, soy silk is considered to be a smooth and intricate fabric, not as durable as linen. One big drawback to soy silk is that it uses formaldehyde in its production. This raises questions regarding its effects on our health and wellbeing and its sustainability.

Banana tences for silk

Bananas are considered to be one of the world's major food crops and are grown in 129 countries. However, it is not the fruit but the stalks which provide the material for creating silk. There are several different methods by which the banana fibres can be collected. These include natural methods, such as manually stripping the plant back using a knife until the fibres are the only thing left. These fibres are then dried and twisted together. Another method might be retting and combing, and some businesses may use chemicals for the extraction of the fibres. It's worthwhile, when selecting this type of fabric, to identify how it was manufactured as some of these methods will have a more harmful impact on the environment. Due to the increased demand for more sustainable and animal-friendly practices, banana silk is becoming more popular and easier to obtain. The fabric is considered to be durable, breathable and biodegradable. It can be made into wool for rugs and carpets or, as identified previously, spun into yarn. However, as it is relatively new, there is a lack of standardization in the industry, meaning it can be hard to track the impact and lifecycle of each product.

Cactus silk

Silk can be manufactured from the Agave Cacti plant. This form of silk production is considered to be sustainable due to the rate at which the Agave Cacti grows. The process involved in making the silk includes pulverizing the leaves and then adding water to separate the fibres. The fibre is then removed, dried and turned into a silk thread. The silk thread can be dyed using natural dyes. Always check that vegetable dyes have been used and not harmful chemicals.

Wool

Woocoa wool

What is this? Woocoa is wool made from both coconut and hemp. It is made by combining both the coconut and hemp fibres, and 'treating them with enzymes extracted from the oyster mushroom' (Livekindly, 2018). The wool was created by some students at the University of Los Andes, Bogota, in Colombia. In 2018, it won a PETA prize for 'Animal-Free Wool'.

Soybean wool

Soybean wool is made from the by-products of the soy food industry. A method called wet spinning is used, in which the soy proteins are removed, dried and then spun into yarn. This process is considered to be sustainable and leaves no waste.

Nullarbor wool

Nullarbor is a wool alternative made from the waste products of coconut. It's transformed into wool by the use of microbes, which turn the waste into microbial cellulose. The manufacturing process is short and sustainable.

Wood cloth/lyocell

Known as lyocell, this fabric is made from either eucalyptus, oak or birch wood. Eucalyptus trees, in particular, are fast growing and do not require pesticides to help them grow. They can also grow in areas where the soil is no longer viable for growing food. The manufacturing process of lyocell requires low amounts of water and energy. Lyocell is made by the wood being transformed into a pulp. This is then dissolved by adding amine oxide, a chemical compound, which creates a raw cellulose liquid. The raw cellulose liquid is then manufactured into a woven fabric. No toxic chemicals are included in the manufacturing process. Because it is a strong fibre, it is generally used in upholstery fabric and mixed with cotton or polyester.

Nettles

Made from stinging nettles, nettle cloth is manufactured in various locations around the world. Green Nettle Textile, located in Kenya, have a nettle growing and eco-fabric manufacturing process which they call 'sustainable sting'. They encourage local communities to grow stinging nettle plantations, which are harvested and turned into a fabric similar to linen. The fibre is extracted from the stalk of the stinging nettle and is then spun into yarn. The yarn is used to make cushions and other products. Green Nettle Textiles use only natural plant dyes to dye their fabric. In 2019, Green Nettle Textile won the Global Change Award. Growing nettles does not require large volumes of water.

Recycled fabrics

Of course, you don't necessarily need to source new fabric for your project. A great sustainable choice would be to recycle fabric or to buy fabrics made from recycled materials.

Re-use and recycle

What lies in the loft? Can you re-use or recycle fabrics within your home for the design project? Re-using and recycling fabric reduces the amount of material which ends up in landfills. If you are unable to re-use it, could you re-sell it or donate it to a charity shop? If you are moving home, maybe you have fabrics such as curtains which do not fit the next property – but they could be left for the new owners or sold on to someone else.

Recycled nylon and polyester

This type of fabric is made from either recycled nylon or polyester. Recycled nylon comes from fishing nets (collected from the world's oceans), old carpets and tights. Recycled polyester is made from recycled plastic bottles. There are two processes for the production of polyester into yarn: 1) the plastic is melted down into yarn; and 2) the plastic is broken down into molecules and then made into yarn. Both types of products are animal friendly and recyclable but not biodegradable. This type of fabric can be considered as adding to the circular economy in a positive manner. Econyl, a product created by the Italian company Aquafil, turns plastic and fishing nets into a nylon yarn. This is then sold and made into new fabric products. Any product made with Econyl yarn will be certified with its branding logo on it.

Top tips: Fabric or upholstered items

➢ *What is the fabric/furniture made of?*

➢ *How is it manufactured?*

➢ *Is it GOTS certified?*

➢ *Is it Oeko-Tex Standard 100 certified?*

➢ *What is the fabric required for (curtains etc.)? Make sure it is suited to the purpose (for example, silk does not like direct sunlight so would not be good in curtains).*

➢ *Is it recyclable or biodegradable?*

➢ *Is it suitable for pets and children?*

➢ *Have you got any fabric in your home you could use/re-use?*

➢ *Does the fabric contain any toxic chemicals?*

➢ *Consider buying second-hand upholstered furniture as this will produce less off-gassing.*

➢ *Will it complement the design?*

Suppliers

Ada & Ina

Located in the United Kingdom.

Available worldwide.

Coyuchi

Located in the United States.

Contact supplier for availability.

Hemp Fabric Lab

Located in Mumbai, India.

Contact supplier for availability.

Higgs & Higgs

Located in the United Kingdom.

Available worldwide.

Myco Works

Located in the United States.

Contact supplier for availability.

Offset Warehouse

Located in the United Kingdom.

Contact supplier for availability.

Piñatex (alternative to leather)

Contact supplier for availability.

The Organic Fabric Company

Located in the United States.

Contact supplier for availability.

Grado Zero Espace

Located in Italy.

Contact supplier for availability.

Part Six
Accessories

Curating the finishing touches to a designed space involves making it personal to you. When accessorizing a space, ask yourself what are the things that interest you: this will help with the choices you make when sourcing your accessories. Other factors to consider include: your chosen design style (will the accessories complement it); where are the items made; are they sustainable and animal friendly; will they promote a circular economy; and will they create a focal point in your design?

Accessories are great at adding an injection of colour or texture, at softening a design or giving it more form and definition. To help accessorize your space, Part Six is broken down into the following: how to successfully accessorize a space; types of accessories; top tips and suppliers of sustainable and animal-friendly accessories.

How to successfully accessorize a space

As with every other element of designing a space, the key with accessorizing is to know what the space is for – specifically, what do you like to do in this space? This is the time to have some fun: accessorize your home with things that reflect you and your personality. I remember when I was a child visiting my grandparents' houses: they seemed like treasure troves, full of lots of exciting things to look at and explore. Ultimately, they were spaces that reflected who they were as people.

Today, there is no end to the number of products available to create the finishing touches to your design. However, it's important to leave some space. Stop and think about why you are buying each item. And of course, when buying accessories, consider the lifecycle of each product you select. What it is made from, how it is made and can it be re-used at the end of its life? Don't just pick everything you like with no plan – instead, try to select objects which will be consistent with the space you're choosing them for. Keep in tune with what reflects you and your personality, or what your business represents if you're decorating an office. Think about the type of ambience you want to create: a minimal, calm and serene space, or a lively, vibrant and modern room? Set the mood and energy of the space *before* starting to select your accessories. When accessorizing a space, consider the visual weight and balance of the objects you are wanting to include. This refers to the colour, size, shape and design of an object.

A great way to include interest and texture in your design is to accessorize with items of varying dimensions and form. For example, you could select three framed pictures of varying sizes and place them together on a desk, sideboard or console table. Selecting an odd number of items will add greater depth, dimension and contrast to your design. If you are accessorizing a small space, consider using only minimal accessories, all large in size (this is known as the cantaloupe theory). You could choose accessories which complement the wall and floor coverings or include antiques within your design.

When selecting colours, start off by choosing items that use colours already used within the design of the space. You could then finish off the design by including a few more accessories of a totally different hue. This will add intrigue and style, creating an eye-catching design. Alternatively, if you want to spice it up and are a fan of all things bold and bright, you could choose accessories of a mixture of hues. This method is great for eclectic and bohemian design styles. However, if you select this option, be sure that the accessories you choose will complement your chosen design style and flow throughout all spaces within your home or work space.

Another option is to colour coordinate your accessories by putting items of the same colour together: for example, reds with reds, blues with blues. This is great when putting books on bookshelves.

Types of accessories

Here are some tips and ideas of different types of accessories you could use to finish off your design.

Ornaments and decorative items

Be selective when choosing accessories. Don't buy them all from one shop; otherwise, your design could end up looking like the inside of that store instead of like a room that is yours. To add additional depth and contrast, include accessories of varying textures, such as cushions, glass vases or ornate marble/stone statues. Don't completely fill up the shelving with books: leave spaces and include ornate and strategically placed accessories. This will add depth, character and style. Additionally, you could lay some of the books down on the shelving to add further intrigue and contrast to the design. Over-filled shelving can make a space look cluttered, creating a stressful effect.

For larger homes or places of work, include bigger objects such as sculptures. Avoid using lots of small accessories in larger spaces as this can create a design which looks cluttered and is not aesthetically pleasing. Add depth and proportion within your living or working space with the inclusion of a mirror. Why not include more than one mirror to make a feature piece on one of the walls? Mirrors have the added benefit of reflecting light around a space, making it look lighter and bigger.

Let's consider now some specific types of decorative items.

Rugs

When selecting accessories for flooring, ensure rugs are made from sustainable and animal-friendly materials. For more information, refer to Part Two, 'Floor coverings'. When selecting a rug for a space, for instance the lounge area, ensure the rug can accommodate the sofas, armchairs and coffee table(s). This will help create boundaries and make the design tidy and flowing.

Plants/flowers

Add some life and colour by including plants. Plants are good for absorbing carbon dioxide (CO_2) and add a happy and uplifting vibe to a space. Plants are known for enhancing our wellbeing.

Artwork

Include some unique pieces of art, like a sculpture. For small spaces, position the artwork at a point furthest from the door. This will make the space look bigger. Hanging artwork should be at eye level unless you are working within an art gallery. Frame artwork with similar colours and styles of frames. Include a mixture of artwork: this will add depth and style whilst creating a design which is aesthetically pleasing to the eye. Adding a unique and monumental piece of artwork can bring a room's interior alive, creating a focal point within the design.

How about creating your own wall of fame, using framed images of you and your family or work colleagues? Use the same type and colour of frame for each photograph. You could even include children's artwork to keep these gems sacred for years to come. Why not include a tapestry made from sustainable and animal-friendly materials? This can be personalized and soften a design.

Antiques

Another great sustainable option is the inclusion of antiques, such as antique pieces of artwork. For these kinds of accessories, explore second-hand shops, antique shops or flea markets. These places can be real treasure troves.

Musical instruments

For music lovers, why not include a musical instrument like a piano? It does not need to be brand new: it could be an instrument which has been passed down from generation to generation in your family or salvaged from an antique or second-hand shop. If you do include a piano, make it a focal point of the space.

Figure 7.8
Copyright of Rachel Fowler Interiors

Soft furnishings

Soft furnishings such as cushions, throws and tapestries are great at adding an injection of colour. When selecting curtains, ensure that they run from ceiling to floor. Ensure you leave enough room either side of a window's width to allow for pulling back the curtains. For varying styles of blinds made from fabric, like Roman blinds, ensure they sit inside of the internal frame of the window. Don't forget: silk fabrics do not like direct sunlight. Mix and match the size of cushions placed on sofas, benches and armchairs. Don't just include a single cushion for the end of each sofa. Be adventurous with the colours: include some bright-coloured cushions so long as this flows with the rest of the design.

Bedding

Bedrooms, of course, will have more soft furnishings than any other space. Let's have a look at finishing off a bedroom design with different kinds of bedding.

Duvets

We all like to snuggle into a cosy duvet, especially in the cooler winter months. There are several different types of sustainable and animal-friendly duvets available, although the most common types are still down and microfibre, which are not. Traditional down-filled duvets are of course not animal friendly, being filled with a type of feather, but not only that: down duvets and pillows are renowned for hiding dust mites and bacteria. Microfibre duvets are made from synthetic fibres and can contain toxic chemicals such as formaldehyde. Alternative duvets to the traditional down duvets include: microgel, TENCEL™ Lyocell and kapok.

Microgel duvets are made from synthetic materials. However, if you look for microgel duvets which display the Oeko-Tex certification, the duvet contains 'no harmful substances and was produced in a sustainable manner' (Of Houses and Trees, 2021).

The Devon Duvets Botanic duvet range is made from fibres containing TENCEL™ Lyocell, which comes from sustainable wood sources. 100% animal-friendly, and the only product of its kind registered with The Vegan Society in the United Kingdom, they contain no synthetic layers, glues or bonding agents. The duvets have moisture-wicking properties, making them a good option for people who might suffer from night sweats, and they are made from biodegradable materials.

Kapok is a material similar to cotton, which comes from the kapok tree. It is a natural, non-toxic fibre.

Pillows

When sourcing pillows, a good rule is to look for those which are made from 100% GOTs certified cotton. These are considered to be breathable, antibacterial and hypoallergenic.

One interesting sustainable pillow filling is buckwheat. Buckwheat pillows originate from Japan. The pillows are stuffed with buckwheat hulls, which is the outside covering of the seed. A great thing about these is that you can wash the outer cover, by emptying the filling out, and then refill the pillow once the outer cover is dry. Buckwheat allows for an airflow, which is good for those who experience hot flushes or who are simply warm at night.

Sheets and duvet covers

Sheets can be made from a range of fabrics with some of the most common being cotton, TENCEL™ fibre or linen.

For cotton bedding, seek out that GOTS certification. 'Dip & Doze', a company based in the United Kingdom, have a Cool and Crisp range, which is ideal for the summertime, warm sleepers or those experiencing hot flushes because the cotton material is lightweight and breathable. Avoid bedding which is non-ironable: this may be a sign that the sheets contain substances such as formaldehyde.

TENCEL™ fibre Ethical Bedding products are made from 100% sustainable Eucalyptus TENCEL™ fibre, harvested from forests protected by the Forestry Stewardship Council certification (FSC). They carry OEKO TEX 100 certification and are the only vegan bedding company in the UK with Vegan Society approval. TENCEL™ fibre bedding is hypoallergenic, hygienic, incredibly breathable, and there are no hidden chemicals.

Linen bedding is made from flaxseed (see Part Five, 'Fabrics'). Linen is strong, breathable and natural.

Throws and blankets

Throws made from 100% natural organic GOTS certified cotton could be a lovely addition to your bedding or chairs. Alternatives for woollen blankets and throws include:

- Hemp woollen blankets;
- Woocoa woollen blankets (mentioned in Part Five);
- Nullarbor woollen blankets/throws (mentioned in Part Five).

If you are after a faux fur style throw/blanket, make sure they are completely animal friendly. This may require you to contact the supplier directly.

Top tips: Accessories

➢ *Buy locally or when on your travels. Ensure it is made ethically and sustainably.*

➢ *Engage with local artists wherever possible.*

➢ *Art students are a good contact for bespoke pieces and will be cheaper than an established artist.*

➢ *Make your children's room personal for them: give it some identity. Make it fun for them. Don't make it the same as the other bedrooms' interiors. Give your children's room character from a child's perspective.*

➢ *Select sustainable and sustainably made ornaments that reflect your personality.*

➢ *Do not make everything match. This could create a design which is flat, not intriguing or stimulating to the eye.*

➢ *Avoid mass-produced items as these are generally made from cheap and potentially toxic materials. If in doubt, contact the supplier.*

➢ *Too many ornaments will make the space look cluttered.*

➢ *Avoid buying from only one big home-furnishing store. Explore second-hand shops, antique shops and flea markets. These places can have some real gems, which will add more character and personality to your design.*

➢ *Be adventurous and add colour with your accessories; make the design look intriguing. Add some glamour.*

➢ *Avoid perfect symmetry. Include varying forms. A variety of shapes will add dimension and style to the design.*

Suppliers (bedding only)

Devon Duvets

Located in the United Kingdom.

Available in the United Kingdom; for the rest of the world, contact the supplier.

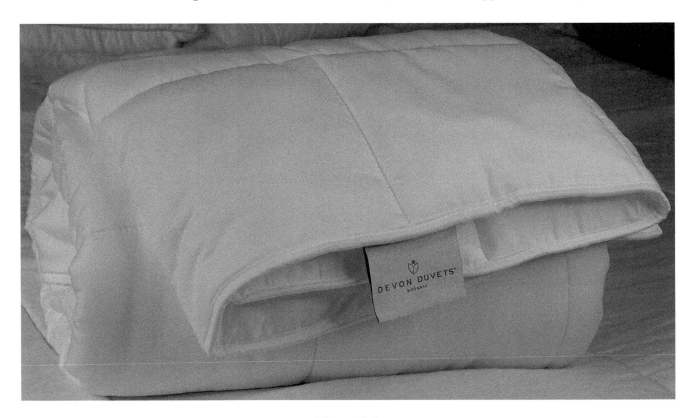

Figure 7.9
Image provided by Devon Duvets
Photographer Pauline Beijen
www.devonduvets.com

Pillows

Comfy Comfy (buckwheat pillows)

Located in the United States.

Contact supplier for availability.

Hullo (buckwheat pillows)

Located in the United States.

Contact supplier for availability.

Natural Bed Company

Located in the United Kingdom.

Contact supplier for availability.

Pine Tales (buckwheat pillows)

Located in the United States.

Contact supplier for availability.

Sachi Organics (buckwheat pillows)

Located in the United States.

Contact supplier for availability.

Bedding

Cotton

ARA Living

Located in the United Kingdom.

Available worldwide.

Coyuchi

Located in the United States.

Contact supplier for availability.

'Dip & Doze' – organic bedding

As 'Dip & Doze' cites, 'All Dip & Doze's bedding is Fairtrade and GOTS certified. To become GOTS certified, harmful chemicals including harsh chlorine bleaches are prohibited. Dip & Doze use low impact, non-toxic dyes and oxygen based whitening products'.

Located in the United Kingdom.

Available only in the United Kingdom.

Figure 8.0
Image provided by 'Dip & Doze'

Figure 8.1
Image provided by 'Dip & Doze'

Green Picks

Located in Germany.

Contact supplier for availability.

Natural Bed Company

Located in the United Kingdom.

Contact supplier for availability.

Oskoe

United Kingdom.

Contact supplier for availability.

Undercover Living

Located in the United Kingdom.

Available worldwide.

TENCEL™ *fibre*

Ethical Bedding

Located in the United Kingdom.

Available worldwide.

Figure 8.2
Image provided by Ethical Bedding

Figure 8.3
Image provided by Ethical Bedding

Undercover Living

Located in the United Kingdom.

Available worldwide.

Linen

SOL Organic

Located in the United States.

Available worldwide.

Part Seven
Infant nurseries

Having a baby is an exciting time. There's so much to do, from ordering the buggy to the big design job – the nursery. Everyone wants to create that dream nursery: a nursery that is mindful and calming, and will have a positive effect on your baby's wellbeing. It's a design project quite unlike any other, which is why it has its own section in this book.

You can spend hours researching nursery design styles, trying to work out what is best. Thankfully, amongst the many materials available, you can find sustainable and animal-friendly products to create a nursery that will meet the health and wellbeing needs of your family, as well as the needs of the environment. Part Seven focuses on the varying elements required in creating the design: wall coverings, flooring, furniture, lighting, soft furnishings and accessories. The part concludes with some top tips to consider when designing a nursery.

How to design a sustainable and animal-friendly infant nursery

Although many of the principles that have already been covered in this book will apply to designing a nursery, there are some specific things to consider when creating a room for an infant. Here is a quick run-through again of the parts of this book, with some specific advice for infant nurseries.

Wall coverings

Colour: Consider neutral tones. Neutral tones create a calming environment for your baby. Avoid intensely dark and bright hues as these can over-stimulate your infant's senses.

Paints: It's about selecting a healthier and safer paint option. I recommend Edward Bulmer Paints 'The Nursery Collection'. See Chapter 1 for more information on plant-based paints.

Figure 8.4
Paint colour: Frankie
Image provided by Edward Bulmer Paints

Figure 8.5
Paint colour: Isabella
Image provided by Edward Bulmer Paints

Wallpaper: Wallpaper can provide character, warmth and personality for your nursery project. Sustainable and animal-friendly wallpaper can be made from: paper sourced from sustainable forests, linen, seagrass, mica, cork, water-based paints, grass-cloth and organic fibres, including coconut bark, Japanese straw and sequoia bark. See Chapter 1 for suppliers.

Flooring

What will create a cosy and warm environment for your baby? A lot of people opt for carpet due to its soft texture but we know from Part Two that carpets are not always healthy and humane. Infants, in their first year of life at least, spend a lot of time on the floor learning to crawl and walk. If carpet is your preferred floor covering option, then choose a carpet made from natural materials that has not been treated, as identified in Part Two. Always make sure that the carpet is installed a few weeks before baby arrives: that way, you can open the windows and allow the space to breathe.

A good alternative option to carpets is wooden flooring with a rug. This can add colour and texture, and soften the design, whilst being easier to keep clean and free of allergens or harmful materials. Vegan and sustainable rugs are available in cotton and banana silk. If you want to add a touch of bohemian style, why not consider organic or recycled cotton rugs. However, when including a wooden floor, ensure the finishes are natural (made from plant-based products) and are low or VOC free.

Furniture

Why not consider using a chest of drawers? This can be super handy for a nursery as it can be used not just for storage, but as a changing table on the flat top. Giving your existing chest of drawers a dual purpose will increase its longevity and reduce the need for new furniture – which is good both for the planet and for your budget.

How about using shelving? This is great for storing books and toys, and for placing pictures on. Adding a children's wardrobe to the design will add to the storage and can grow with your child's needs. A mirror can be a nice touch as babies like to look at their reflections. And why not complement the design with a bespoke comfy chair for those cosy intimate bonding moments of feeding and cuddles?

Now for the cot or crib. With such a wide variety available, what things should you be looking out for to promote a positive and healthy sleeping environment for your baby? Think about sustainability through reusability of the cot. Consider buying a cot which can turn into a toddler bed. Remember to identify what has been used to finish the furniture. Try to identify paints and finishes that are plant or water based and are low or VOC free. If this is not advertised on the product, contact the supplier for further information. Look for furniture which is Forestry Stewardship Council (FSC) certified.

Selecting a healthy, sustainable and animal-friendly mattress can seem like a treasure hunt: you're looking for a mattress which is non-toxic and contains natural and organic materials. Be careful when looking for an animal-friendly cot mattress because some natural cot mattresses contain wool. Cottonsafe® Natural Mattress in the United Kingdom offer a vegan cot mattress, which they advertise as completely chemical free and animal friendly. Remember to allow time for the mattress to air after being unwrapped from its packaging.

Figure 8.6
Image provided by Getty Images

Lighting

To promote the health and wellbeing of your baby, use fun light fittings that will create a serene and tranquil environment. Avoid bright lighting as this may be over-stimulating for your baby's senses. Choose warm and soft LED bulbs for the nursery. A grand ornate circular lampshade for a ceiling light might look great, but how will this affect your baby? Be creative with the lighting. Choose a ceiling light which is fun, oversized and adds to the theme of the design. Don't forget to use a dimmer switch for the ceiling light. This will enable you to come in in the middle of the night to do any changes or feeds without overwhelming your baby's senses. You could also create a layered lighting design for a harmonious and aesthetically pleasing effect. For instance, you could use a ceiling light, wall lights and a table lamp. Avoid floor lamps – once your infant starts exploring (crawling and walking), they could pull it over. Ensure all lights are out of the reach of little fingers. Don't forget to include a night light, making those night-time feeds less of an assault course of dodging furniture and toys. Create a space which promotes harmony and a peaceful sleep for your baby.

Soft furnishings

In promoting a happy and healthy environment for your baby, be sure to include a duvet, blankets and pillows which are GOTS certified 100% organic cotton and have not been exposed to any chemicals. This ensures the product is both socially and responsibly made, from harvesting to finished item. For example, Oskoe organic cotton cot bed duvet is GOTS certified. Avoid rayon bamboo fabrics as these contain chemicals. For window dressings, use black-out curtains and blinds to keep the room dim and cool during daylight and summer hours. Black-out curtains are made from layers of fabric woven together to block out more light than a standard curtain fabric. But note that some black-out blinds can contain polyvinyl chloride, a toxic chemical. Beware of greenwashing: a product may be advertised as organic, but does it have the certification to back it up?

Accessories

Add a personal touch to the nursery but take care not to clutter the space. A cluttered space could over-stimulate your baby and may not feel relaxing. Avoid too those small items that are attractive to young hands and could end up in their mouth, nose or ears. Include things which complement the design of the room. Photographs on the wall are a good option; but you should avoid hanging anything heavy on the walls in case it falls. Include wooden toys and even a mini table and chair. Avoid plastic wherever possible and ensure that all wooden products have the FSC logo and are not finished in toxic chemicals. There are lots of great ways to make your nursery look cosy and fun, but always check what the products are made from. Ensure they are healthy and animal friendly.

Figure 8.7
Copyright of Rachel Fowler Interiors

Top tips: Infant nurseries

➤ *Paint the walls, ceiling and woodwork well in advance; no paint is completely VOC free and you want to give the room time to air.*

➤ *Ensure the carpet is installed a few weeks before your baby is due and ventilate the room once installed.*

➤ *Look at Auro for plant-based and low-VOC wooden floor finishes/lacquers.*

➤ *Look at Cottonsafe® Natural Mattress for chemical-free and animal-friendly infant and children's mattresses (certified by the Vegan Society).*

➤ *Ensure good space planning.*

➤ *For cots, think sustainable – consider a cot which will turn into a bed.*

➤ *Don't clutter the nursery with too many things.*

➤ *Enjoy creating this space for the new member of your family.*

Resources

Here is a directory of the sustainable and animal-friendly suppliers that were available at the time of writing. There may be even more around, and Google is always a good friend for these questions – but hopefully here is a very good place to start!

Sustainable and animal-friendly wall coverings

Paint

Auro Natural Clay Paint	+ 44 1544 388 332
www.auropaint.co.uk	
Earthborn Paints	+ 44 1928 734171
www.earthbornpaints.co.uk	
Edward Bulmer Paints	+44 1544 388 535
www.edwardbulmerpaint.co.uk	
Eico	+ 44 845 073 9432
www.eico.co.uk	
Francesca's Paints Ltd	+ 44 207 228 7694
www.francescaspaint.com	
Graphenstone	+ 34 955 529 435
www.graphenstone.com	
Pure & Original	Unknown
www.pure-original.com	

Wallpaper

Glamora – Glampure Range +39 320 494 7716
www.glamora.it/en/glampure
Rachel Fowler Interiors +44 752 820 0486
www.rachelfowlerinteriors.co.uk

Tiles

Bert & May +44 203 744 0776
www.bertandmay.com
Fireclay +1 800 773 2226
www.fireclaytile.com
Fornace Brioni Cotto +39 0376 58142
www.fornacebrioni.it/en/
Iris Ceramica Tiles +39 0536 862340
www.irisceramica.com
Maitland and Poate + 44 203 983 3631
www.maitlandandpoate.com
Mandarin Stone (natural stone tiles) + 44 160 071 5444
www.mandarinstone.com
Salvatori (natural stone tiles) +39 0584 769200
www.salvatoriofficial.com/en/can-we-help/contact-us/
Vintage Floor Tile Company +44 123 385 0082
https://thevintagefloortilecompany.co.uk

Clay plaster wall covering

Clayworks +44 132 634 1339
https://clay-works.com

Cork

Puretree Cork – Organic Blocks +44 139 284 9116
https://puretreecork.com/products/wall-cork/organic-blocks

Mushroom wall coverings

Mogu https://mogu.bio/	Unknown

Wood products

Encore Reclamation www.encorereclamation.co.uk	+44 207 001 7605
Foresso https://foresso.co.uk	+44 203 302 7387
Scumble Goosie+44 145 373 1305 https://scumblegoosie.co.uk/	

Sustainable and animal-friendly flooring

Wood

Foresso https://foresso.co.uk/	+44 203 302 7387
Hargreaves Reclaimed Wood Flooring www.hargreavesreclaimedflooring.co.uk	+44 132 483 2200
Lassco Wooden Flooring www.lassco.co.uk/flooring/	+44 207 394 2100
Reclaimed Flooring Company	+44 207 250 1108 (UK) +1 800 683 6943 (USA)
www.reclaimedflooringco.com/	

Carpet/rugs

Sisal and Seagrass www.sisalandseagrass.co.uk/	+44 208 558 0887

Tiles

Bert & May	+44 203 744 0776
www.bertandmay.com	
Fireclay	+1 800 773 2226
www.fireclaytile.com	
Fornace Brioni Cotto	+39 0376 58142
www.fornacebrioni.it/en/	
Iris Ceramica Tiles	+39 0536 862340
www.irisceramica.com	
Maitland and Poate	+ 44 (0)203 983 3631
www.maitlandandpoate.com	
Mandarin Stone	+ 44 (0)160 071 5444
www.mandarinstone.com	
Salvatori (natural stone)	+39 0584 769200
www.salvatoriofficial.com/en/can-we-help/contact-us/	
Vintage Floor Tile Company	+44 (0)123 385 0082
https://thevintagefloortilecompany.co.uk	

Natural Stone (flooring and wall covering)

Corradini Group	+39 045 6269 455
https://corradinigroup.it/en	
Heritage Stone Company	+44 193 929 0690
https://heritagestonecompany.co.uk	
Landford Stone	+44 179 432 4232
www.landfordstone.co.uk	
Mandarin Stone	+ 44 160 071 5444
www.mandarinstone.com	
Natural Stone Online	+44 190 460 7675
www.naturalstone.co.uk	
Salvatori	+39 0584 769200
www.salvatoriofficial.com/en/can-we-help/contact-us/	
UK Slate	+44 153 955 9289

www.slate.uk.com

Venice Marble +44 208 795 4625
https://venicemarble.co.uk/

Sustainable furniture suppliers

Bolia +45 88 96 02 26
https://design.bolia.com

Brdr Kruger (Denmark) +45 39 56 15 55
www.brdr-kruger.com

Cottonsafe® Natural Mattress +44 139 523 9832
(vegan and sustainable)
www.cottonsafenaturalmattress.co.uk

José Manuel Carvalho Araújo Not available
www.carvalhoaraujo.com

Konk Furniture +44 117 329 4114
https://konkfurniture.com

Mater Design +45 70 26 44 88
https://materdesign.com

Norm Architects +45 28 87 93 09
https://normcph.com/

Ottan Studio +90 536 361 20 11
www.ottanstudio.com

Sebastian Cox +44 208 316 5679
www.sebastiancox.co.uk

Tom Raffield +44 132 672 2725
www.tomraffield.com

Infant bedroom furniture

CottonSafe® Natural Mattress +44 139 523 9832
(vegan and non-toxic certified mattresses)

Green Cradle +1 (877) 476 2735
www.greencradle.com/collections/solid-wood-cribs

Naturalmat	+44 1392 877 247
www.naturalmat.co.uk/nursery/furniture	
Oeuf	+1 (718) 965 1216
https://oeufnyc.com/collections/cribs/products/sparrow-crib	
Poppy's Little Treasures	Not available
www.poppyslittletreasures.com/collections/cots/products/pre-order-the-airlie-cot	
www.cottonsafenaturalmattress.co.uk	

Sustainable lighting suppliers

Asano Japanese lighting	
(available from a number of online retailers)	
AY Illuminate	+31 33 457 1486
www.ayilluminate.com	
Bicycle Glass	+1 833 245 4448
www.bicycleglass.com	
Brdr Kruger	+45 39 56 15 55
www.brdr-kruger.com	
Cerno	+1 949 715 1534
https://cernogroup.com	
David Trubridge	+64 6 650 0204
https://davidtrubridge.com/nz/	
Gray pants	+31 20 820 8990
www.graypants.com	
IRUSU Candles	Not available
www.irusu.co.uk	
Nuddy (vegan candles)	Not available
www.nuddy.co.uk	
Octó Candles	Not available
https://octoandco.com/	
Recycled/antique chandeliers	
(from a reputable supplier or antique store)	
Slamp	+39 06 916 2391
www.slamp.com	

Tom Raffield   +44 1326 722 725
www.tomraffield.com
WU lamp made of rice paper
(available from a number of online retailers)

Sustainable and animal-friendly fabrics

Ada & Ina   +44 207 183 7986
www.linenfabrics.co.uk
Coyuchi   +1 888 418 8847
www.coyuchi.com
Hemp Fabric Lab   +91 22 249 12554
https://hempfabriclab.com
Higgs & Higgs   +44 145 375 0660
www.higgsandhiggs.com
Myco Works   Not available
www.mycoworks.com/
Offset Warehouse   Not available
www.offsetwarehouse.com
Piñatex   +44 207 257 9371
www.ananas-anam.com/
The Organic Fabric Company   Not available
www.organicfabriccompany.com
Grado Zero Espace   +39 517 80368
www.gzinnovation.eu/section/11/materials

Accessories

Pillows

Comfy Comfy   Not available
https://comfycomfy.com/collections/buckwheat-pillows
Green Fibres   + 44 180 386 8001
www.greenfibres.com/product/317/pillows.htm

Green Picks	Not available
www.greenpicks.de/en/	
Hullo	+1 877 334 8556
https://hullopillow.com/buckwheat-pillow	
Natural Bed Company	+44 114 272 1984
www.naturalbedcompany.co.uk/product/organic-cotton-kapok-filled-pillows/	
Pine Tales	Not available
www.pinetales.com	
Sachi Organics	Not available
www.sachiorganics.com/products/bw-test-2	

Duvets

Devon Duvets	+44 175 234 5399
www.devonduvets.com	
Green Fibres	+44 180 386 8001
www.greenfibres.com/product/319/duvets.htm	
Natural Bed Company	+44 114 272 1984
www.naturalbedcompany.co.uk/2019/06/03/vegan-bedding/	

Bedding

Alterra Pure	+1 805 285 3639
www.alterrapure.com/	
ARA Living	+44 208 360 8304
https://araliving.com	
Cam Cam Copenhagen	+45 88 74 23 01
https://camcamcopenhagen.com	
Coyuchi	+1 888 418 8847
www.coyuchi.com	
Dip & Doze	+44 161 537 1797
www.dipanddoze.com	
Ethical Bedding	+44 782 187 6914
https://ethicalbedding.com	

Green Picks	Not available
www.greenpicks.de/en/home-living/home-textiles/organic-bedding/iaio-organic-bedclothes-satin-pure-3-part-bedding-set-kingsize-for-2.html	
Natural Bed Company	+44 114 272 1984
www.naturalbedcompany.co.uk/2019/06/03/vegan-bedding/	
Oskoe	Not available
www.oskoe.com	
SOL Organic	+1 952 829 0400
https://solorganix.com/collections/duvet-collection	
Undercover Living	Not available
https://undercoverliving.com	
Under the Canopy	+1 833 328 8246
https://underthecanopy.com	

Infant bedding

Burts Bees Baby	+1 855 540 2229
www.burtsbeesbaby.com	
Cam Cam Copenhagen	+45 88 74 23 01
https://camcamcopenhagen.com/collections/blankets	
Green Fibres	+44 180 386 8001
www.greenfibres.com/product/322/bedding-for-children.htm	
Infant & Child Bedding, Cocoon Company	+45 40 49 11 49
www.cocooncompany.dk/en/produkt-kategori/sleeping-products/bedding/	
Kapok Baby Duvet (pram & cot), Cocoon Company	+45 40 49 11 49
www.cocooncompany.dk/en/produkt-kategori/sleeping-products/duvets/	
Kapok Carry Cot Mattress, Cocoon Company	+45 40 49 11 49
www.cocooncompany.dk/en/produkt/kapok-madras-til-lift/	
Scandiborn (blankets)	Not available
www.scandiborn.co.uk/collections/blankets-1	
The Little Green Sheep	+44 178 973 4020
www.thelittlegreensheep.co.uk/bedding/	

Sustainable and animal-friendly certifications

Other than the ones referenced throughout the book, here is a list of sustainable and animal-friendly certifications to look out for. At the time of writing, these are the ones you want to see on products you choose.

BREEAM

A sustainability assessment tool used in the design and build of buildings.
www.breeam.com

British Allergy Foundation Seal of Approval

Endorsement scheme for a wide range of products.
www.allergyresearch.co.uk/seal-of-approval

Certified Vegan

Contains no animal products.
https://vegan.org/certification

Climate Neutral

Certifies your product to PAS 2060 (a specific guideline on how to create a carbon-neutral product/business).
www.climateneutral.org/

Cradle to Cradle Certified (CM) Products Program

A product made is done so with sustainability used in its design.
www.c2ccertified.org

CRI Green Label

Certifies rugs and carpets for low-VOC emissions.
https://carpet-rug.org/testing/green-label-plus/

EPEAT

Global registry for greener electronics.
www.epeat.net/

Fairtrade

Fairtrade is an ethical trade system that puts people first.
www.fairtrade.net/

Forestry Stewardship Council (FSC)

Wood is sourced from either sustainable forests or from post-consumer waste. (Certification includes: 100% FSC certified or FSC and Mix certification).
https://fsc.org

Global GreenTag Certified

All products have been tested to meet the standards set out by Global GreenTag.
www.globalgreentag.com

Global Organic Textile Standard (GOTS)

Certifies that the product is made from organic fibres. This includes the complete manufacturing process, from harvesting to sustainable responsible manufacturing processes.
www.global-standard.org/

Green Guard

Certifies products used for inside spaces, for instance materials used in an interior or architectural design project, have been 'scientifically proven to meet third party chemical emissions standards (VOCs), helping reduce indoor air pollution' (UL, 2021).
https://spot.ul.com/greenguard/

Green Seal

Paints. Lifecycle-based sustainability standards.
https://greenseal.org

Green Tick

Independent sustainability certification of products or services.
www.greentick.com/

Leaping Bunny

Cruelty free.
www.leapingbunny.org

LEED

Leadership in Energy and Environmental Design Certified.
A sustainable/green rating system in the design and build of buildings.
www.usgbc.org/leed

Low VOC

Products contain low levels of volatile organic compounds.

Oeko-Tex

Textiles have been tested for harmful substances, from its raw material to its finished product.
https://www.oeko-tex.com/en/

Rediscovered Wood Certification

Furniture made from recycled wood.
www.rainforest-alliance.org/business/issues/forests/how-does-the-rainforest-alliance-work-with-nep-con/

SCS Indoor Advantage

Products meet indoor air quality.
www.scsglobalservices.com/

SCS Sustainable Choice

Carpets and rugs meet measurable environmental performance and social responsibility criteria.
www.scsglobalservices.com/

Vegan Society Trademark

A registered charity which provides information and certifies products as being humane.
www.vegansociety.com/

Zero Waste to Landfill

Certifies that a company has an audit trail to demonstrate that its waste is being disposed of in a positive manner, therefore not ending up in a landfill.
https://zwia.org

Bibliography

42 Floors. (2020). *What's a LEED Certification, and How Do You Get LEED Certified?* [Online]. Available from: https://42floors.com/edu/beyond-the-basics/what-is-a-leed-certification-and-how-do-you-get-leed-certified [Accessed: 20 September 2020].

About Organic Cotton.org. (2016). *What is Organic Cotton?* [Online]. Available from: http://aboutorganiccotton.org [Accessed: 5 September 2020].

Balogh, A. (2020). *What Makes Concrete a Sustainable Building Material?* [Online]. Available from: www.concretenetwork.com/concrete/greenbuildinginformation/what_makes.html [Accessed: 25 May 2020].

C2 Certified. (2020). *What is Cradle to Cradle Certified®?* [Online]. Available from: www.c2ccertified.org/get-certified/product-certification [Accessed: 1 May 2020].

Chechar, L. (2019). *How to Accessorize Your Home Like a Pro.* [Online]. Available from: https://dengarden.com/interior-design/How-to-Accessorize-Your-Home-Like-a-Pro [Accessed: 20 September 2020].

Clayworks. (2020). *Sustainability.* [Online]. Available from: https://clay-works.com/sustainability/ [Accessed: 30 May 2020].

Concrete Network. (2020). *Concrete Sustainability.* [Online]. Available from: www.concretenetwork.com/concrete/greenbuildinginformation/ [Accessed: 1 June 2020].

Conestoga Tile. (2015). *Why Ceramic Tile is Environmentally-Friendly.* [Online]. 1 April 2015. Available from: www.conestogatile.com/why-ceramic-tile-is-environmentally-friendly/ [Accessed: 30 May 2020].

Devon Duvets. (2020). *Where It All Began, Our Story.* [Online]. Available from: www.devonduvets.com [Accessed: 25 November 2020].

Earthborn Paints. (2020). *Hello. We're Different, Just Like Our Paints.* [Online]. Available from: https://earthbornpaints.co.uk/about/ [Accessed: 10 May 2020].

Edward Bulmer Paints. (2020). *Why Our Paint.* [Online]. Available from: https://www.edwardbulmerpaint.co.uk/paint-conscience [Accessed: 10 May 2020].

Ellen MacArthur Foundation. (2017). *Concept. What Is a Circular Economy? A Framework for an Economy that is Restorative and Regenerative by Design.* [Online]. Available from: www.ellenmacarthurfoundation.org/circular-economy/concept [Accessed: 5 May 2020].

Ethical Bedding Company. (2020). *Organic Eucalyptus Tencel Bedding.* [Online]. Available from: https://ethicalbedding.com/collections/frontpage [Accessed: 20 November 2020].

Ferreira De Sa. (2020). *Our Commitment to the Planet.* [Online]. Available from: www.ferreiradesa.pt/newsdet.php?i=228 [Accessed: 1 June 2020].

Foresso. (2021). *Ethical Manufacturing.* [Online]. Available from: https://foresso.co.uk/ethics. [Accessed: 1 January 2021].

Forest Stewardship Council. (Unknown). *Who We Are.* [Online]. Available from: www.fsc-uk.org/en-uk/about-fsc/who-is-fsc [Accessed: 20 May 2020].

Fornace Brioni. (Unknown). *Company. Creative Director.* [Online]. Available from: www.fornacebrioni.it/en/company/ [Accessed: 30 May 2020].

Fungially. (2018). *What is Mycelium: Nature's World Wide Web Underneath Our Feet.* [Online]. Available from: https://fungially.com/what-is-mycelium-natures-world-wide-web/ [Accessed: 7 September 2020].

Garagnon, E. (2020). *Ethical Silk Alternatives: Citrus Fibre and Vegan Spider Silk.* [Online]. 16 March 2020. Available from: https://goodonyou.eco/ethical-silk-alternatives/ [Accessed: 25 January 2021].

Global Organic Textile Standard (GOTS). (2016). *The Standard.* [Online]. Available from: www.global-standard.org/the-standard.html [Accessed: 5 September 2020].

Green Nettle Textile. (2019). *Home of Eco-Friendly Textiles.* [Online]. Available from: http://greennettletextiles.com [Accessed: 17 September 2020].

Home Guides. (2020). *Green Alternatives to Foam in Upholstery.* [Online]. Available from: https://homeguides. sfgate.com/green-alternatives-foam-upholstery-98187.html [Accessed: 20 August 2020].

Lewis Bamboo. (2020). *Why Bamboo? (Green Solution).* [Online]. Available from: https://lewisbamboo. com/pages/why-bamboo-green-solution [Accessed: 20 August 2020].

Little Greene. (Unknown). *Frequently Asked Questions.* [Online]. Available from: www.littlegreene.com/ paint-faqs [Accessed: 1 May 2020].

Livekindly. (2018). *Students Awarded for Creating Cruelty-Free Vegan Hemp and Coconut 'Woocoa' Wool.* [Online]. Available from: www.livekindly.co/cruelty-free-vegan-hemp-coconut-woocoa-wool/ [Accessed: 18 September 2020].

Maitland and Poate. (2020). *Antique Encaustic Tiles.* [Online]. Available from: www.maitlandandpoate.com/ our-story/ [Accessed: 1 June 2020].

Martin, T. (2018). *Warm Light Bulbs vs Cool Light Bulbs: Which Should You Buy?* [Online]. Available from: www.cnet.com/home/smart-home/should-you-buy-warm-or-cool-lights/ [Accessed: 5 April 2021].

Mavolu. (2018). *Fabric from Food Waste: Soy Fibre for Fashion and Textiles.* [Online]. Available from: https:// mavolu.com/blogs/news/fabric-from-food-waste-soy-fibre-for-fashion-and-textiles [Accessed: 15 September 2020].

Mavolu. (2018). *From Waste to Value: Banana Fibre for Fashion and Textiles.* [Online]. Available from: https:// mavolu.com/blogs/news/from-waste-to-value-banana-fibre-for-fashion-and-textiles [Accessed: 20 September 2020].

McDarris, A. (2020). *Sustainable Fabrics: Lyocell – What is Lyocell.* [Online]. Available from: https://terradrift. com/sustainable-fabric-facts-lyocell-what-is-lyocell-is-lyocell-sustainable/ [Accessed: 15 September 2020].

Mogu. (2021). *Mogu Facts.* [Online]. Available from: https://mogu.bio/faqs/ [Accessed: 25 January 2021].

Muller & Son. (2029). *Lotus Silk – Yarn from Buddhas Flower.* [Online]. 28 December 2019. Available from: www.muellerundsohn.com/en/allgemein/lotus-silk/ [Accessed: 25 January 2021].

Muratto. (2016). *Five Reasons to Consider Cork in Interior Design.* [Online]. Available from: www.muratto.com/ en/newspress/1-general/2-five-reasons-to-consider-cork-in-interior-design [Accessed: 30 May 2020].

National Institute of Environmental Health. (2020). *Flame Retardants*. [Online]. Available from: www.niehs.nih.gov/health/topics/agents/flame_retardants/index.cfm [Accessed: 11 November 2020].

Nicholson, K. (2018). *22M Pieces of Furniture Thrown Out Every Year in the UK*. [Online]. Available from: https://resource.co/article/22m-pieces-furniture-thrown-out-every-year-uk-12892 [Accessed: 1 July 2020].

Octó Candles. (2020). *About*. [Online]. Available from: www.octolondon.com/pages/about [Accessed: 3 August 2020].

Oeko-Tex. (2020). *Our Standards*. [Online]. Available from: www.oeko-tex.com/en/ [Accessed: 25 September 2020].

Of Houses and Trees. (2021). *3 Cruelty-Free Duvet Options for Vegans and Animal Lovers*. [Online]. Available from: www.ofhousesandtrees.com/vegan-bedding/ [Accessed: 26 March 2021].

Ogundehin, M. (2020). *Happy Inside*. London: Ebury Press.

Oskoe. (2018). *Organic Cotton Cot Bed Duvet*. [Online]. Available from: www.oskoe.com/collections/duvets-pillows/products/odeja-organic-cotton-cot-bed-toddler-duvet [Accessed: 19 October 2020].

Palmwood. (Unknown). *Environmental Credentials*. [Online]. Available from: www.palmwood.net/environmental-credentials/ [Accessed: 1 June 2020].

Pinatrex. (2017). *Inspiration*. [Online]. Available from: www.ananas-anam.com/about-us/ [Accessed: 6 September 2020].

Pritchard, A. (2019). *Let's Cosy Up: Why You Need to Embrace Organic Linen*. [Online]. Available from: https://pebblemag.com/magazine/living/why-you-need-to-embrace-organic-linen [Accessed: 13 September 2020].

Savvy Rest. (2020). *Does Memory Foam Contain Toxic Chemicals?* [Online]. Available from: https://savvyrest.com/info/does-memory-foam-contain-toxic-chemicals [Accessed: 1 July 2020].

Schimdt, J. (2018). *Fungi Power: The Mushrooms Replacing Leather in Eco-friendly Fashion*. [Online]. Available from: https://en.reset.org/blog/fungi-power-mushrooms-replacing-leather-eco-friendly-fashion-11122018 [Accessed: 8 September 2020].

Slamp. (2021). *Slamp the Leading Light*. [Online]. Available from: www.slamp.com/en/materials/ [Accessed: 10 September 2020].

Smith, K. (2018). *Students Awarded for Creating Cruelty-Free Vegan Hemp and Coconut 'Woocaoa' Wool.* [Online]. Available from: www.livekindly.co/cruelty-free-vegan-hemp-coconut-woocoa-wool/ [Accessed: 17 September 2020].

Souza, E. (2019). *How Lighting Affects Mood.* [Online]. Available from: www.archdaily.com/922506/how-lighting-affects-mood [Accessed: 2 September 2020].

TCPI. (2020). *The Psychological Impact of Light and Color.* [Online]. Available from: www.tcpi.com/psychological-impact-light-color/ [Accessed: 2 September 2020].

The Spruce. (2019). *Is Bamboo Flooring Really Eco-Friendly? Bamboo is Renewable and Biodegradable but Still Has Some Concerns.* [Online]. Available from: www.thespruce.com/is-bamboo-flooring-really-eco-friendly-1314953 [Accessed: 1 June 2020].

Tile Devil. (2018). *Are Tiles Environmentally Friendly?* [Online]. Available from: https://tiledevil.co.uk/blogs/style/ceramic-porcelain-tiles-environmentally-friendly?_pos=7&_sid=98d1bcfb9&_ss=r [Accessed: 1 June 2020].

UL. (2021). *UL Green. Guard Certification Program.* [Online]. Available from: www.ul.com/resources/ul-greenguard-certification-program [Accessed: 10 January 2021].

Urbanline Architectural. (2018). *Hardwood vs Softwood: Pros, Cons, and Best Uses.* [Online]. Available from: www.urbanline.com.au/hardwood-vs-softwood-pros-cons-best-uses/ [Accessed: 20 May 2020].

Use Natural Stone. (2016). *Top Five Reasons Why Natural Stone is a Sustainable Choice for Your Home.* [Online]. Available from: https://usenaturalstone.org/top-five-reasons-natural-stone-sustainable-choice-home/ [Accessed: 20 May 2020].

Vritti Designs. (2016). *Nettle Fabric – Hand Made from Himalayan Stinging Plant.* [Online]. Available from: https://vrittidesigns.com/handwoven-himalayan-nettle-fabric/ [Accessed: 20 September 2020].

Wood Products. (2014). *Wood Construction Reduces Stress and Offers a Healthy Living Environment.* [Online]. Available from: www.woodproducts.fi/articles/wood-construction-reduces-stress-and-offers-a-healthy-living-environment [Accessed: 25 May 2020].

Acknowledgements

Writing a book was something which I had never thought or dreamed that I, Rachel Fowler, would ever be able to achieve – especially due to having dyslexia. However, helping and promoting the health and wellbeing of people is something which has always been very important to me. Being able to switch careers from a nurse into the world of design and still being able to continue with this passion fills me with a great sense of pride and personal achievement – even if I am now working for health in a different way. Until speaking with clients, friends and family, I did not realize how little people know about sustainable and animal-friendly design, and the effects that design materials could be having on their lives and the environment.

I started writing this book in the front bedroom of my parents' house, after getting stranded in the UK during the COVID-19 pandemic. It was so great to have the support and encouragement of my parents and to be able to involve them in this process.

This experience has been tough and challenging, but with the additional support of the No Bull Business School (Sarah Akwisombe and Jennifer MacFarlane) and my business coach Paula Ashby, it has been a great experience.

Writing this book has made me step out of my comfort zone, contacting companies and hoping that they would be able and willing to help me. Therefore, I would like to thank all those wonderful companies who took time out of their busy schedules to email or talk with me on the telephone. It was great to communicate with so many like-minded businesses.

Lastly, I would like to thank my wonderful loving husband, who spent Christmas 2020 proofreading my book and supporting me through this process, even though at times I think I just confused him.

Home, a place
where memories are made.

&

work, a place to create who
you want to be.

Thank you for reading